I dedicate this book to my wife,
Carol, whose patience and support
were vital to its creation.

A Great Lakes Treasury of Old Postcards

LAKE SUPERIOR

GEORGIAN BAY

Canadian Harbour Scenes, 1894 - 1960

LAKE HURON

LAKE ONTARIO

Lorenzo Marcolin, MD

LAKE MICHIGAN

LAKE ERIE

First Edition

Cover design, layout and typography by Kurt Harding Schick.
All Great Lakes maps by KHS, © 2007
Printed on 50% recycled paper by Rose Printing in Orillia, Ontario.

Library and Archives Canada Cataloguing in Publication

Marcolin, Lorenzo, 1932-
A Great Lakes teasury of old postcards : Canadian harbour scenes,
1894-1960 / Lorenzo Marcolin.

Includes bibliographical references.
ISBN 978-0-921922-19-3

1. Harbors--Great Lakes Region (North America)--Pictorial works.
2. Great Lakes Region (North America)--Pictorial works.
3. Great Lakes Region (North America)--History.
4. Postcards--Great Lakes Region (North America)--History. I. Huronia Museum II. Title.
F551.M37 2007   971.3'00222   C2007-905638-5

To order copies of this book, please contact:
Huronia Museum, 549 Little Lake Park Road, P.O. Box 638, Midland, ON, L4R 4P4
Phone: **705.526.2844** Email: **info@huroniamuseum.com** Website: **www.huroniamuseum.com**

Contents

A Short History of Postcards 6
Introduction 7
Acknowwledgments and Credits 10

Chapter 1
Lake Superior to Sault St. Marie 11
Fort William 11
Port Arthur 19
Jackfish 27
Montreal River 28
Sault Ste. Marie 28

Chapter 2
Northern Georgian Bay to Port Severn 39
Bruce Mines 40
Blind River 40
Little Current 41
Manitowaning 42
Killarney 42
South Bay Mouth 44
Point au Baril 48
Parry Sound 49
Depot Harbour 53
Honey Harbour 54
Minnicognashene 57
Port Severn 58

Chapter 3
Southern Georgian Bay to Owen Sound 59
Waubaushene 60
Victoria Harbour 61
Port McNicoll 61
Midland 71
Penetanguishene 85
Collingwood 90

Thornbury 96
Meaford 97
Owen Sound 98

Chapter 4
Wiarton, Tobermory and Lake Huron 107
Wiarton 108
Tobermory 109
Port Elgin 111
Kincardine 111
Goderich 112
Point Edward 114
Sarnia 115

Chapter 5
Lake St. Clair and Lake Erie 119
Wallaceburg 120
Walkerville 121
Windsor121 121
Chatham 125
Erieau 127
Port Stanley 128
Port Burwell 129
Port Dover 129
Port Colborne 130
Crystal Beach 134

Chapter 6
Niagara and Lake Ontario to Kingston 135
Niagara Falls 136
Welland Canal 136
Queenston 139
Niagara on the Lake 139
Lewiston 140
Port Weller 140

Contents

Port Dalhousie 141

St. Catharines 140

Grimsby 142

Hamilton 143

Toronto 144

Port Hope 152

Cobourg 153

Trenton 153

Belleville 154

Picton 156

Kingston 157

Chapter 7
St. Lawrence River to Montreal   **159**

Gananoque 160

Brockville 161

Prescott 161

Cornwall 163

Lachine Rapids 165

Montreal 169

References and Bibliography   **175**

A Short History of Postcards

The hobby or business of collecting post-cards is called Deltiology. In 1861, a John P. Charliton of Philadelphia obtained the first patent for a postcard in the USA. The first postcard to be sent via a mail service was in Austria in 1869. The idea was that a simple message on a postcard would be cheaper than using a letter enclosed in an envelope. In 1895, the US government began selling "postal cards" that were cheaper than private postcards, because they already had a stamp affixed to the card, which was included in the price; the private cards required the purchaser to buy his stamp separately. No message was allowed on the back of the card, which was reserved for the address. In 1898, a government Act eliminated the difference between the government "postal cards" and private cards, and from then on the mailing of postcards increased markedly. From c.1900 to 1907, the back of the card was still limited to the address only. Government legislation starting on March 1, 1907, allowed the back of the

card to be divided, allowing one half for the address and the other half for a message. Some companies did not immediately put in the dividing line. I suspect that they waited for their already printed inventory to be sold. The introduction of the dividing line on the back of the card helps with the dating of a card, but is not totally fool proof.

From the turn of the 19th century, Germany printed most of the postcards. This lucrative industry came to an end with the advent of World War I. After the war, both the USA and England began to produce many postcards. In 1893, some of the earliest postcards produced in the USA advertised the World Columbian Exposition in Chicago (The Chicago World's Fair). Most of these postcards were of the Exposition buildings. After this, Exposition sales of postcards in the USA took off. In 1908, over 675 million cards were mailed in the USA alone.

After World War I, the "white border" era began, with the border around the picture. Many people wrote their message in the white border space. This style lasted until about 1930. In 1930, the "Linen" card was introduced and lasted until 1945. These cards were printed on paper that resembled cloth or linen. It was less expensive to print on these textured postcards. One could print them using cheaper inks, and they had a certain brightness to them. There are many ways to classify postcards. One might consider different countries, forms of transportation, Christmas scenes, animal types, advertising cards, art deco, art nouveau, locations, artist-signed cards and many more. The French, earlier in this century, were well known for erotic cards! Real photo cards seem to be the type that is in demand and warrants a higher price today.

Introduction

The first postcard book that I know about depicting marine scenes and boats of the Great lakes was published in 1976. It was a small volume with photos of 152 postcards and was authored by Bob Welnetz. The project was sponsored by the Manitowoc Museum in Manitowoc, Wisconsin. It is not clear if the postcards featured by Mr. Welnetz were owned by him or if some of them were the property of card owners who allowed their postcards to be used in the book. The author thanked various individuals for their "help in assembling the cards and data." Mr Welnetz indicated that practically all the data "under" the postcard photo was taken from the actual card. Where possible, he added some information.

Late in 1977, Mr Welnetz came out with a second volume that was different from Volume 1. Beneath each card's description, he gave appropriate credit and indicated from whose collection the card came from. Six of the cards in that volume were from my collection.

Over the years, my collection has grown into the thousands. Having been born and raised on Georgian Bay, I always had an interest in the Great Lakes, especially in the boats, shipping activity and history. All during high school, college and even medical school, I worked as a waiter on the CPR boats out of Port

McNicoll. After graduating from the University of Toronto in medicine and training in orthopaedic surgery in Cleveland, Ohio, I began a private practice in Maryland near Washington, DC. By the early 1970s, I was very busy with my orthopaedic practice and did not have the time to attend many postcard shows where I could purchase postcards for my collection. Therefore, in order to expand my collection, I decided to use "pickers." These are people, often retired, who love postcards and at postcard shows go through on assignment, checking probably hundreds of cards at the display tables. They are looking for the postcards requested by the collectors. A separate, special fee was never charged me, but the picker was rewarded by purchasing the cards, usually at a discount, and then selling them to a buyer like me, and in this way made his profit. The picker would probably add a premium to the price he paid to the vendor, which in turn he passed on to me. I do not believe the pickers made a lot of money; it was rather a labour of love for them! At one time, I had five pickers who regularly sent me postcards on approval. I would select the ones I wanted and would return the rejects with my cheque, which included the postage. I would only purchase Great Lakes cards. Often the pickers would send me cards that were not of the Great

Lakes; I would reject these cards after research revealed that they were from New England, Hudson River, California coast and other places. After a while, the pickers knew which boat cards they should send me. I would purchse all Great Lakes cards except where there were duplicates. The duplicate had to be appreciably better than the one I had before I would buy it. Occasionally, I would reject a postcard that at that time I thought was outrageously priced. Some of these cards were "real photos" of ship launchings. I now regret that I did not buy all of them, because I now know that these cards have appreciated tremendously in value and now are selling at a great premium, even more than the regular, real photos of boats.

Over the years, the pickers dropped off and I was left with a single picker; a gentleman from Massachusetts, who faithfully sent me cards on consignment every few months for years. Our relationship was strictly business and I never spoke with him. After many years, his return address changed to a retirement community in Texas. Then there was a second Texas address. This was followed with a return address in Florida. Many months later, a packet of cards arrived with the return address of a woman with the same last name; I presumed it was his widow. The last postcard approval packet arrived in the fall of 2006! This relationship had lasted over 30 years.

I used pickers for the bulk of my acquisitions, but after retiring from medical practice I have been able to attend a few postcard shows to continue buying for my collection. My collection goes back over 42 years. I can truly say that not only was I a medical specialist, but also a postcard specialist; but only of Great Lakes postcards!

When I began to think about doing a book on Great Lakes postcards, I thought I would do all of the Great Lakes, both in Canada and in the USA. After reviewing my collection, I realized this would be a monumental task. I would end up with a very large tome, too big for a normal sized coffee table! Also, I knew that I was much more familiar with Canadian harbour scenes, having sailed into several of them, and, over the years, driven by car into the rest of them. Except for Cleveland, Ohio, where I lived for four years, and a few other ports that I had visited, I was not familiar with the majority of the American ports.

If you compare the Canadian population living along the shores of the Great Lakes with its American counterpart, you will find a ratio of one to six; there are six times more Americans living along the Great Lakes than Canadians. The American "big" cities situated on the Great Lakes are Chicago, Green Bay, Milwaukee, Detroit, Cleveland, Buffalo, Rochester, Toledo and others. On the Canadian side, we have the metropolises of Toronto and Montreal. Only two other cities, Thunder Bay City and Hamilton, have fairly substantial populations. So it was a simple choice to confine this volume to Canadian harbours and end up with a reasonably sized book.

I decided to plan the volume in a orderly geographical fashion by starting at the Lakehead. This would be the relatively "new" city of Thunder Bay City, which became a reality in 1970 with the amalgamation of the original Fort William and Port Arthur. I felt that I could begin there and then trace my way down the north shore of Lake Superior to Sault Ste. Marie, Ontario, St. Mary's River, then along the North Shore of Georgian Bay to include Manitoulin Island. Then down the eastern shore of Georgian Bay via Parry Sound to Port McNicoll, Midland, Penetanguishene, Collingwood and Owen Sound. After Tobermory, I continued along the Canadian shore of Lake Huron to the St. Clair River,

Lake St. Clair, and then on to the north shore of Lake Erie. After traversing the Niagara River and Gorge, I arrived at Lake Ontario. I then followed the northern shore of Lake Ontario to Kingston. This leg would include Toronto, Hamilton and several smaller ports. Then I passed along the St. Lawrence River to Montreal via Prescott and Cornwall. I decided to include Montreal because, although not really part of the Great Lakes, it was the most important harbour receiving grain from the Canadian West via rail and the Great Lakes. Also, Montreal was and still is one of the main ports for loading other products onto ships for shipment to Europe. As well, it was the main passenger terminal for immigrants coming to Canada, and for travellers going to Europe from Canada.

I recall, during World War II, the off-loading of products from Milwaukee and Chicago at Port McNicoll for transhipment by rail via Smith Falls to Montreal. The main products were baled cotton and large sacks of green coffee beans. I believe these products were for the war effort. The CPSS *Alberta* and CPSS *Athabaska* had been taken out of "mothballs", so to speak, to carry out this new venture. They had been tied up at Port McNicoll during the depression until World War II. You could guess that the government was not taking any chances of losing such important products destined for the war effort. German U Boats were very active along the American Eastern Seaboard during the war, looking for easy prey. Obviously, it was safer to ship products such as cotton and coffee inland via the Mississippi River to Lake Michigan and then on to Montreal, than up the eastern seaboard.

You will note that there are more cards of Georgian Bay than of the other regions. As a native of Port McNicoll on Georgian Bay, I had probably searched more diligently for these. Over the years, I visited many times all the harbours of Georgian Bay and became familiar with them. You will find that some harbours and places in this presentation are not well represented. For example, a Wasaga Beach postcard is not included. The reason could be that tis town did not have an actual dock area where larger craft such as passenger boats or small freighters could dock. As well, most of my collection was accumulated over 42 years while I was living in the USA. Wasaga Beach is well known to Ontario natives as a summer tourist beach area, but is virtually unknown to Americans in the eastern part of the USA, so very few American tourists would visit the town, and few cards would have been mailed to the States. Also, I avoided just beach scenes and tried to obtain cards that had boats at dock or leaving or arriving in the harbour. Although Hamilton, Ontario, is quite a large city, I have only two cards showing the "piers". Most Hamilton postcards that I found were of the steel mill and not of the harbour. I concluded that the city was not in the past a primary tourist and recreational destination, and so marine postcards of this city would be comparatively rare.

Until twenty years ago, I would purchase practically every Great Lakes postcard that was sent to me, both in colour or black and white. At that point, I decided to concentrate on real photos only and preferably only cards prior to 1950.

Postcard collecting has become very popular and one might say it has become "big business." It is obvious that at postcard shows most of the collectors specialize in a specific subject. I never met anyone else who specialized exclusively in the Great Lakes. Many collected ocean ships, trains, railway stations and various other transportation subjects. At one point, I placed an ad for one year in a popular postcard magazine asking specifically for Great Lakes boat postcards, and never received a single response. Over the years, I have perused very carefully the so-called mail auctions in postcard magazines and internet auction sites and have found very few Great Lakes postcards that I could use in my collection. In recent years, one can find some Great Lakes postcards on the commercial website eBay, but very few are "antique." After Bob Welnetz's two volumes of "Great Lakes on Postcards," I never came across a similar book until in 2001, when a volume appeared by Sally Sue Witten entitled "Lake Erie Ports and Boats in Vintage Postcards," published by Arcadia Publishing Co. of Chicago; it is a part of a series called "Postcard History Series." The volume covers scenes from Windsor to the Welland Canal on both the American and Canadian sides, but seven of 27 Canadian cards were not of boats or actual harbour scenes.

Working on this volume has been interesting and enjoyable. The research took a lot of time, using many websites and rereading many of the books on the Great Lakes that are in my library. The volume has 305 photos of boats and/or harbour scenes. Of these cards, half are originally in colour, and the remainder in black and white, or combinations of black and white with colours decorating the periphery of the card, or sepia tones.

The author plans to donate the profits from the sales of this book to the Huronia Museum in Midland, Ontario, after retrieving his initial costs.

Acknowledgements and Credits

I want to thank my wife Carol Ann for her support and encouragement during the 42-year collection of material for this book. Also appreciated was her help going to postcard shows and looking through hundreds of cards in order to find a few Great Lakes cards which I did not yet have in my collection. A thank you to Scott Cameron, Trustee of the Owen Sound Marine Museum, for the use of several postcards from their collection. Scott and I go way back when we worked together as summer help on the C.P.S.S. *Assiniboia*. Sincere thanks also to Jamie Hunter, Director of the Huronia Museum in Midland, Ontario, for his encouragement to do this volume and for the use of postcards from the Huronia Collection. These cards were mainly of Georgian Bay, many by J.W. Bald, the best-known photographer of Georgian Bay scenes. Thanks are also due to my son Joseph for doing some of the proof reading of the text and the excellent improvements he suggested. I would be remiss if I did not thank the several "pickers" years ago, who sent me cards on approval; the most dependable were a couple, the Petersens from New England, and more recently Florida, who began sending me cards more that 30 years ago. Just this past fall I received a packet on approval from Patricia Petersen. I also want to thank all the many unknown photographers, whose work has made this volume a treasury of Great Lakes images. I leave to the last, my most sincere thank you to Kurt Harding Schick, book designer extraordinaire, who came highly regarded and whose diligence, experience and originality will show itself in this volume; this past spring he was honored with the Fred Langton Award from the Ontario Historical Society for the best regional history in Ontario for the past three years.

CHAPTER 1

Lake Superior to Sault St. Marie

Fort William • Port Arthur • Jackfish • Montreal River • Sault Ste. Marie

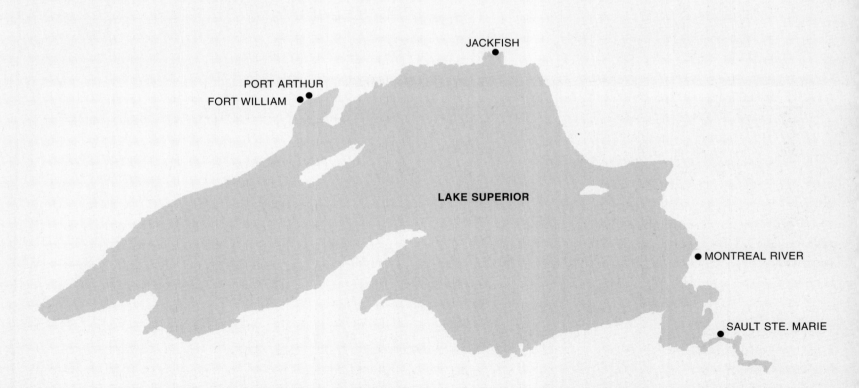

Elevators, Fort William, on Canadian Pacific Railway

Post mark 1906. View on the Kaministiquia river showing three grainers loading at three different elevators; the closest one belongs to the CPR (Canadian Pacific Railway) company. Fort William was established in 1798 after moving from a Grand Portage site. This original site had been in a dispute between USA and Canada. Fort William was named after William McGillivary, the Northwest Company's chief superintendent at that time.

Post mark is 1909. This grain elevator complex is identified as "Ogilive's (misspelled) Mill and Elevator." The first Ogilvie's mill was built in 1906 but possibly due to improper foundation slipped into the river. The Ogilvie family had come from Great Britain to Canada in the 19th century and already were well known as millers. Actually, the company passed out of the family in 1902, when the two Ogilvie men who ran it, died. The company changed hands and merged several times, until it was purchased by Labatts beer company. Finally it was purchased by Archer Daniels Midland Co. of Decatur, IL.

Ogilive's Mill and Elevator, Fort William, Ontario.

No post mark. This card is from a painting, not a photograph. It appears to be an advertising card issued by the Grand Trunk Railway Co. The Grand Trunk Pacific Railway was a wholly owned subsidiary of the Grand Trunk Railway Co., but it was almost totally funded by the Canadian Government. It remained as a separate entity from 1907 until 1916, when it went into receivership and became part of the Canadian National Railway system. The location is on the Kaministiquia River.

Another view of the Kaministiqua River. The third vessel in the row appears to be a CPR boat probably the *Alberta* or the *Athabasca* at the CPR freight shed. At that time they were still sailing out of Owen Sound.

No post mark. This view is looking up the Kaministiqua river. It shows five boats at dock and two moving up the river. Note Mt. McKay in the left background. The second boat at dock probably is either the *Alberta* or the *Athabasca*.

Harbour, Fort William, Ont., Canada

Another view on the Kaministiqua River at Fort William looking west up the river. In the background is Mt. McKay. Photo was taken about 1914. The first fur trading post was established on Thunder Bay at this site in 1683.

Harbour View, Fort William, Ont., Canada

MOUNT McKAY SHOWING KAMINISTIQUIA RIVER AND SWING BRIDGE NEAR FT. WILLIAM, ONT. CAN.

No post mark. This is a good view of Mt. McKay, the Kaministiqua River and the area west of Fort William. The photo was probably taken during the 1940s.

This panoramic view of the harbour along the Kaministiqua River in Fort William. Note dated on reverse of card is Aug. 2, 1915, so the photo was taken before that time. Eleven boats can be seen. Just past the grain elevators on the left side of the photo, one can make out the *Keewatin* or *Assiniboia* while they were still painted black; a second ship is probably one of the smaller sister ships also painted black, the *Manitoba*.

The Harbour, Fort William, Ont., Canada

C. P. R. Elevators, Fort William, Ont., Canada.

Post mark is 1920. Another scene along the Kaministiqua River with eight boats being visible at or near the CPR grain elevator complex.

Card is entitled " Opening of Navigation" at Fort William; it shows several grainers, with ice still visible on the surface of the Kaministiqua River. Photo was probably taken late April. No date recorded. (Card stock and print quality very poor.)

Opening of Navigation, Fort William, Ont., Canada.

No post mark. This is CPR elevator `D', again on the Kam River. There are three boats waiting to be loaded with grain.

C. P. R. Elevator "D," Fort William, Ont., Canada.

CANADIAN NATIONAL RAILWAY ELEVATOR (THE LARGEST IN THE WORLD), NEAR FORT WILLIAM, ONT., CANADA.

No post mark. This grain elevator is referred to as the "largest in the world"! I believe soon after, a larger one was built in Brazil. This elevator complex was really between the "twin cities" of Port William and Port Arthur, facing open water. This is the only card not showing the Kam River. The grain boat at the elevator is the *William A. Reiss* built in 1925; it grounded in 1935, was declared a total loss, and scrapped.

The postmark is 1907. This card shows the CNR dock with two vessels at dock and one at the CPR dock. The photo was taken prior to 1907, so if the boat on the left is a CPR boat, it most likely sailed from Owen Sound, which was still the company's main Bay Port. Port Mc-Nicoll became the CPR's main port in 1912.

C. N. R. Docks, Port Arthur, Ont.

Water Front, Port Arthur, Ont.

Postmarked is 1909. View is of the CPR dock and, to the right, the CSL dock. The boat at end of the CSL dock is the *Huronic*. The boat at the CPR dock is probably the *Alberta* or its sister ship, the *Athabaska*.

Postmarked is 1911. This is another view of the CPR and CNR docks at Port Arthur. Later on, the dock to the right would be known as the CSL dock. The two closest boats are small grainers. The vessel on the right, second row, is a passenger boat. The second-row vessel at the CPR dock is a wooden schooner. Note "Sleeping Giant" in the background.

Postmark is 1911. This is a card printed by the CPR and was available to its passengers. It is a panoramic view of Port Arthur.

This is an interesting card showing a boat ready to be launched. The boat is identified as the *J.T Home*. It appears to be a large tug. Date of launch is May 10, 1913. The photo is by a local photographer, "Rogers' Studio" in Port Arthur.

No postmark. This is a rare photo of Port Arthur with the upper photo showing the city and the Port Arthur Hotel, CPR station and pagoda. Many Port Arthur cards are similar to the lower photo, showing the dock area. Port Arthur and Fort William amalgamated on June 1, 1970, and became the City of Thunder Bay. Prior to amalgamation, the two cities were often referred to as "The Lakehead".

Postmark is 1918. This photo was taken from the roof of a freight shed on the dock at Port Arthur. It shows a partial view of the *S.S. Hamonic* at dock. In the background is the impressive Prince Arthur Hotel.

No postmark. This card shows probably the *Assiniboia* docked at the CPR dock and, a few feet away at the CNR dock, probably the *Huronic*. The automobiles suggest that the photo was taken during the 1920s. (Card stock and print quality are very poor.)

No postmark. This is a composite view of Port Arthur, Ontario, showing a mansion, a summer camp, a hotel and the *Noronic* and *Assiniboia* docked. Since the *Assiniboia* is painted black, this photo was taken before 1922. The postcard seems to be promoting a "scenic auto highway" between two Port Arthurs, one in Texas and the other in Ontario. I am certain that such a route never became popular!

AT PORT ARTHUR, ONTARIO—The Place to Spend a Vacation.

The Beginning of the Great Mississippi River Scenic Auto Highway "Port Arthur, Ontario, to Port Arthur, Texas."

Elevator Group at South End of City, Total Capacity 7,000,000 Bushels, Port Arthur, Ont.

Photo by Lovelady, Port Arthur.

The postmark is 1923. This view shows the group of elevators situated between Port Arthur and Fort William. Photo is from about 1920. Note the steam dredge at work.

The Largest Elevator in the World (Capacity, Ten Million Bushels), Port Arthur, Ont., Canada

No postmark visible, but a short message is seen. The stamp on the reverse shows King George V. His reign was from 1911 to 1936. Thus, this card could be from any one of those years, but is most likely from the early 1930s.

No postmark. The interesting fact that there are no boats at any of the elevators suggests the photo was taken prior to the start, or after the end of the shipping season. Many of the elevators have disappeared, not only at Thunder Bay but also on Georgian Bay and the lower lakes. With the large diesel engines, the grain can be shipped directly to Montreal and East Coast ports. The more powerful engines can now haul over the Rockies. During the late summer months and early fall, shipping can go through Fort Churchill (now renamed Hudson Bay City) on Hudson Bay and then by ocean ships directly to foreign ports.

GENERAL VIEW OF ELEVATORS, (TOTAL CAPACITY OVER 20,000,000. BUSHELS), PORT ARTHUR, ONT., CANADA.

23

Port Arthur, Ontario, Canada. —37.—C.P.R. Photo.

Postmark is 1941. This appears to be a free advertising card printed by the CPR. It was available in all the writing desks on board all the CPR boats plying the Great Lakes. This view was taken from the very front of the top deck of either the *Keewatin* or the *Assiniboia*, overlooking the front of the promenade deck. The red brick and white stone building is the Prince Arthur Hotel. The dock area of Port Arthur was a very popular site for a postcard view. This view is reversed, showing the downtown area instead of the harbour.

No postmark. This view shows a boat at the CNR dock, probably the *Huronic* or *Hamonic*. Most likely this is a card printed during World War II.

View of Port Arthur, Ontario, Canada. —10.

A real photo, postmarked 1951. It shows the *Prindoc* of the Patterson line loading grain at one of the grain elevators. This probably is a commercial card ordered by "Hilltop Cabins" and was free to their patrons.

HILLTOP CABINS.   GRAIN ELEVATOR PORT ARTHUR

No postmark. This view is of the *Keewatin* and *Hamonic* docked together at Port Arthur. The *Hamonic* burnt in 1946, so this photo was taken before that date. As a young member of the summer crew working on the *Keewatin*, I remember this exact docking position of these two boats. This would be a Thursday morning after the *Keewatin's* arrival; the *Hamonic* was already docked. After unloading a few passengers and some freight, the *Keewatin* departed for Fort William and would leave there on Saturday for the return trip to Port Mc-Nicoll, arriving there on Monday. The schedule of the *Assinboia* would be the reverse.

No postmark. Port Arthur had one of the major shipyards and drydock on the Great Lakes. One can see from this photo that the drydock has the capacity for handling much larger vessels. The boat in the drydock cannot be identified.

A real photo of roof tops of port Arthur, but more importantly, it is one of best views that I have seen of the "Sleeping Giant," which is not an island but a peninsula. Years ago, when I worked on the CPR boats, this always had to be explained to the passengers. From the deck of a boat, especially when leaving Fort William, it appeared to be an island. On the other hand, the "Giant's Tomb" in Georgian Bay is an island.

Fishing Village, Jack Fish, Lake Superior   On Canadian Pacific Railway

Sepia photo taken before 1904. Jackfish is located off Highway 17 on the north west shore of Lake Superior about 20 miles from Terrace Bay. It is now a ghost town. During the building of the CPR main line west, the village sprung up. In 1895, a 600-foot trestle was built over its excellent harbour, so coal boats could unload coal for the CPR locomotives. Later, fishing became a major industry. With the arrival of the lamprey eel in the early 1960s, this industry died out.

Post mark is 1910. This card is further testimony that Jackfish was a commercial fishing center. With the CPR mainline passing through, fish could be packed in ice, shipped by train and arrive in large centres such as Toronto and Montreal as "fresh fish!"

Drying Nets, Jack Fish, Lake Superior

27

No post mark. Real photo of Str. *Meteor* docked along the bank of the Montreal River. Photo is probably from the 1920s. Two of the male passengers are wearing bowler hats!

No postmark. Since the copyright was registered in 1902, the card was probably published soon after that date. The title of the card is "Pulp Mills and Algoma Iron Works, Sault Ste. Marie, Ont."

6518. PULP MILLS AND ALGOMA IRON WORKS, SAULT STE. MARIE, ONT.   COPYRIGHT, 1902, BY DETROIT PHOTOGRAPHIC CO.

No post mark. The view refers to the Clergue Industries which had been started by the American entrepreneur Francis Hector Clergue. Clergue arrived in the Canadian Soo in 1894 and his industries were bankrupt in 1903. This photo had to be taken between those years and more than likely closer to 1903, because the industries all appear functioning. They included a pulp and paper mill, (later Abitibi Pulp and Paper) and a steel plant (later Algoma Steel). The white vessel to the right is most likely the *Minnie M*, which was the Algoma Steamship passenger boat. In spite of his bankruptcy, Clergue should be considered the "father" of the Sault Ste. Marie industrial base.

General View of Clergue Industries Lake Superior Corporation, Sault Ste Marie, Canada.

BESSEMER STEEL PLANT, SAULT STE. MARIE, ONT., CANADA.

Post mark is 1907. The card is a view of the Bessemer Steel Plant started by Francis Hector Clergue prior to 1903. After Clergue's bankruptcy, this plant eventually became known as the Algoma Steel plant.

Postmark is 1909. The photo is a nice mix showing two large ore carriers or grainers, with two older, smaller vintage steamboats probably close to being phased out.

FREIGHTERS WAITING TO ENTER LOCKS, SAULT STE. MARIE, ONTARIO

"THE EMPIRE UPON WHICH THE SUN NEVER SETS."

COPYRIGHTED 1904 BY ATKINSON BROS.

This card is embellished with maple leaves in colour. The postmark is 1905 and the photo was copyrighted in 1904, when it was probably taken. It was obviously a popular photo, still appearing years later on a postcard.

Birds-eye view of American Locks, showing semi-centennial naval parade, August 2nd and 3rd, 1905. Sault Ste. Marie. No. 1822 S. W. Kirvan, Publisher. Made in Germany.

Postmark is 1906. Very interesting and unusual photograph. The title of the card is self-explanatory. There are eleven boats in the photo.

No postmark. Printed in Great Britain. A boat covered with ice, probably after having traversed Lake Superior, always made an interesting post card. It would point to the danger that accompanied late fall trips on the Great Lakes!

The Last Boat of the Season at Sault Ste. Marie, Ont., Canada

The End of Navigation, Sault Ste. Marie, Canada

This early, Canadian produced card pictures a small bulk carrier covered with ice, probably a very late arrival to Soo from the Lakehead. By the contoured ice flowing over the sides one wonders if it is a whaleback? The inset black and white photo is surrounded by colourful provincial flags.

This card is post marked 1907. It shows four boats locking down in the Canadian locks. They are ready to exit downbound. It was a situation similar to this when the *S.S. Assiniboia* was ready to be lowered 22ft. to the level of the lower St. Mary's River. This level was reached by letting the water out from the lock when the *Perry Walker* struck the gates, allowing the *Assiniboia* to enter the lower St Mary's river without really "locking through!"

"Ship Canal, Sault Ste Marie, Canada"

The boat in the Canadian lock is the *Keewatin* or the *Assiniboia* locking through to Lake Superior. This is a postcard of an artist's series commissioned by the Canadian Pacific Railway Company to illustrate scenes form their transportation system in Canada. The artist was G. F. Gillepsie, a British artist who also did paintings of the CPR ocean liners. These postcards were available free to the passengers at all writing desks aboard and in the barber shop.

C.P.R. Steamer " Keewatin " passing through the Canal, Sault Ste. Marie, Ont.

Gates of Locks at Sault Ste. Marie, Ontario, Canada, after being carried away June 9th, 1909.

Postmarked is 1910. Taken soon after the incident when the *S.S. Assiniboia* accidently passed from the higher level of Lake Superior 22 feet down to the level of the St Mary's River. The mishap took place on June 9, 1909. The *S.S.Assiniboia* was tied to the dock in the lock when the *Perry G. Walker* of the Gilchrist Fleet accidently ran into the gate of the lock, allowing the water to cascade down. This caused the *Assiniboia* to break free and the *Crescent City*, which was behind her to exit as well. The *Perry G Walker* grounded on a shoal down stream and the *Assinboia* had minimal damage. Only the *Crescent City*, loaded with iron ore, had a bad ending and sunk in shallow water near the Soo's Michigan side.

Postmark is not clear, but it looks like 1908 or 1909. Since the *Hamonic* was launched at Collingwood in 1908 for the Northern Navigation Line, this would be a photo when the boat was quite new. It is seen downbound from Lake Superior. When it was launched, it was the largest passenger boat in Canada. It burnt while docked at Point Edward in 1945 with no loss of life due to the quick acting captain.

Northern Navigation Co.'s Steamer "Hamonic," passing through the Locks, Sault Ste. Marie, Ont., Canada

Probably the most popular postcard on the Great Lakes after Niagara Falls are the locks at Sault Ste Marie, both Canadian and American. This card shows the *S.S. Huronic*, sistership to the ill-fated *S.S. Noronic*. The *Noronic* burned at dock in Toronto in early September 1949.

P-136. SOO, ONT. "HURONIC" IN LOCK.

This card shows the Sault Ste. Marie International Bridge with a view towards Canada. Prior to the bridge opening on October 31, 1962, the only connection between the two Sault Ste. Maries was a railroad bridge and a ferry service.

Postmark is 1943. This real photo shows the *Samuel Mather* downbound via the American ship canal just prior to entering the locks. The *Samuel Mather* was launched in 1927 at Lorain, Ohio, for the Interlake Steamship Co. Eventually, it was sold Canadian, changed it's name twice and finally was sold for scrap in 1988.

No post mark. The photo is that of the *Michipicoten* docked at the government dock at Sault Ste. Marie. This boat was originally built as the *E. K. Roberts* at Detroit. It changed ownership twice and was last owned by the Owen Sound Transportation Company, which changed the name to *Michipicoten*. The *Michipicoten* carried freight to North Channel ports and to the Soo from Owen Sound. It burnt in 1917.

The postmark is 1937. This view shows more than 20 boats awaiting the opening of the locks at Sault Ste. Marie, Canada. It appears that these boats are below the locks waiting to lock through to Lake Superior. Although the postmark is 1937, this photo is from a much earlier time.

Opening of Navigation, Sault Ste. Marie, Canada.

No postmark. This is a strange card showing the old blockade house which was part of the original fort constructed by the Hudson Bay Company. Why the photographer would want to include three "tame" bears doing tricks is hard to understand, except if he wanted to make the card more interesting so it would sell better! This is the same blockade house that Francis Hector Clergue restored and lived in for several years when he first moved to the Soo from Maine.

Old Blockade House of Hudson Bay Co., Sault Ste. Marie, Ont., Canada.

No postmark. This card from the early 1960's shows the passenger boat *South American* entering the ship canal at the Soo. In the background is the International Bridge built in 1962. The bridge was a cooperative effort between the State of Michigan and the Canadian federal government. Previously, border crossing was done by ferries and a railroad bridge built in 1880.

C. P. R.
Great Lakes Steamer
in Canadian Lock
At Sault Ste-Marie.

The boat in the Canadian lock
Keewatin or the Assiniboia locki
Lake Superior. This is a postcard of a
commissioned by the Canadian Pa
Company to illustrate scenes form the
tion system in Canada. The artist was
a Briton who also painted the CPR
These postcards were available free to th
at all writing desks aboard ship and i
shop.

CHAPTER 2

Northern Georgian Bay to Port Severn

**Bruce Mines • Blind River • Little Current • Manitowaning • Killarney
South Bay Mouth • Point Au Baril • Parry Sound • Depot Harbour
Honey Harbour • Minnicognashene • Port Severn**

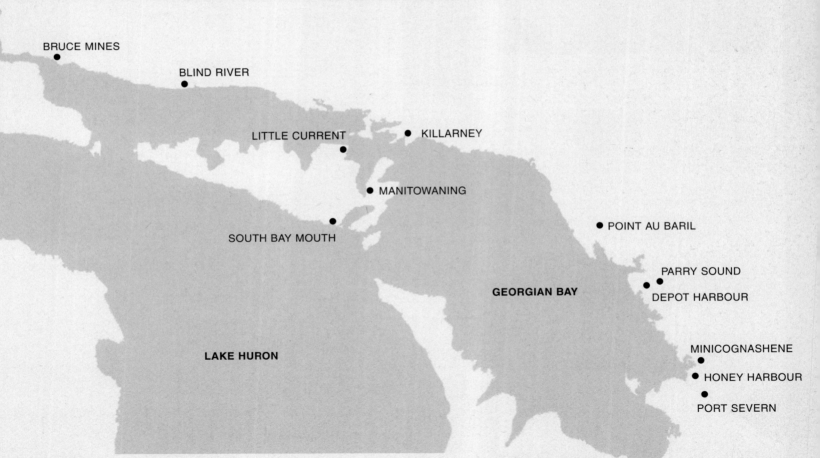

BRUCE MINES

BLIND RIVER

LITTLE CURRENT

KILLARNEY

MANITOWANING

SOUTH BAY MOUTH

POINT AU BARIL

PARRY SOUND

DEPOT HARBOUR

GEORGIAN BAY

MINICOGNASHENE

HONEY HARBOUR

PORT SEVERN

LAKE HURON

Steamer Germanic, Bruce Mines, Ont..

054

No postmark. The boat in the distance is identified as the steamer *Germanic*, therefore the card is from around 1907, plus a year or so. The boat is approaching the harbour at Bruce Mines past the long pier. This community was established in 1846 at site of a large copper deposit. Many of the original miners were Cornish. It was the first incorporated town in northern Ontario.

No postmark. This is a real photo of Blind River located on the North Channel of Georgian Bay between Sault Ste. Marie and Sudbury. The community around a saw mill which was built in that location. The photograph appears to be taken from the smoke the saw mill. There is no evidence of any motor which makes me believe that this photo was taken 1910.

VIEW FROM SMOKE-STACK, CARPENTER-HIXON CO.
BLIND RIVER. ONT.

Card is dated 1907. It shows three boats docked and two under power; one appears to be arriving and the other one is departing. Little Current was a busy little port. Many of the smaller steamboats from Midland, Collingwood, Owen Sound and Parry Sound came here. I have not identified all of these boats, but I am sure local historians could easily do this. The boat leaving could be Northern Navigation Company's steamer *Germanic*.

Sept. 30, 1907.
Ella.

Harbor
Little Current

Little Current, Manitoulin Island, North Channel, Georgian Bay

Postmark is 1907. This is a panoramic view of the harbour. Little Current was first settled in the 1860s. It became an important lumbering centre and then a popular tourist destination. Often the docks would be busy with both passenger boats and lumber hookers. Little Current is situated on the northeastern shore of Manitoulin Island, where the island is closest to the mainland.

41

Postmark is 1932. This card shows the *Caribou*, a small passenger boat that carried passengers and freight from Owen Sound and other southern Georgian Bay ports to ports along the north channel, including Manitowaning, as far as Sault Ste. Marie. The village was incorporated in 1837 as a centre for contact with the Indians. It was a major port on the island. Now it is the site of the *Norisle* Heritage Museum with the *Norisle* as the centre piece. The *Caribou* was built in Goderich in 1904. It ran the so-called "turkey trail," carrying passengers and livestock from Owen Sound to Manitoulin Island until 1946.

Caribou in Manitowaning, Bay, Ont.

No postmark. Unusual vi[...] idyllic, near Killarney. The [...] produced for the Grand Trunk [...] and was probably used by the r[...] advertising purposes. Most like[...] provided free to passengers w[...] their transportation system.

A Charming Vista near Killarney, North Channel, Georgian Bay

Killarney Harbour

No postmark. This is an early view of Killarney Harbour, probably about 1920. There is one passenger steamboat, probably leaving for southern ports on Georgian Bay. For many years, there would be regularly scheduled boats travelling between Owen Sound and Killarney. The small steamboat under way was probably one of these.

No postmark. This is a panoramic view of Killarney with a boat at dock, probably the *City of Collingwood*, *Germanic* or *Majestic*. Killarney is situated on the north channel of Georgian Bay. Its original Indian name meant "canoe passage." The site was a well-travelled route for the Indians, French fur traders, voyageurs, explorers and missionaries. The first trading post here was established in 1820 by a Frenchman. In 1874, Lady Dufferin, wife of the Governor General, changed the name to Killarney. Through-out the years it was an important port for trading, logging, fishing, mining and finally tourism. Passenger-carrying steamships regularly stopped here.

Killarney Channel, Ont., Canada

Killarney, Ont.

No postmark. This is a [...]
from the early 1950s. [...]
situated on the north shor[e...]
Bay. It went by its Ojibway [...]
bahonaning, which means [...]
sage". A fur trading post w[...]
in 1820. The name was [...]
Killarney in 1854, and no-[...]
know why. Like in a lot of t[...]
munities on Georgian Ba[...]
was an important early indu[...]
by fishing. Until 1962, the [...]
Killarney was by water; in [...]
highway was put through.

No postmark. The Steamer *Manitoulin* was one of the early boats carrying both passengers and automobiles to the north channel of Georgian Bay, disembarking passengers, freight and autos at her ports of call, including South Bay Mouth. The autos in the photo appear to be models of the 1930s.

44

No postmark. Another view of the *S.S. Norisle* approaching South Bay Mouth. This card is similar to the card below and was probably taken at the same time, in the late 1940s.

S. S. NORISLE   SOUTH BAY MOUTH, ONTARIO

No postmark. This is a real photo of the *S.S. Norisle* approaching South Bay Mouth on the south shore of Manitoulin Island. The *Norisle* started in service in 1946 and was retired in 1974. She is now docked at the small village of Manitowaning, where she made many dockings during her active period. The Canadian Government has spent much money establishing the *S.S. Norisle* Heritage Museum; the boat is being completely restored.

S. S. NORISLE   SOUTH BAY MOUTH, ONTARIO

S. S. NORISLE   SOUTH BAY MOUTH, ONT

No postmark. This real photo sho
Norisle approaching the dock a
Mouth on Manitoulin Island. She
Collingwood in 1946, the first boat bu
after World War II. The engines were i
Canadian destroyer, but since the wa
they were placed in the Norisle. Along
ter ships, the M.S. Norgoma and the
they provided the ferry service betwee
Mouth and Tobermory. They were repl
by the much larger M.S. ChiCheemaun,
sailing today.

No postmark. This photo was probably taken during the 1960s. South Bay Mouth is on the south shore of Manitoulin Island and is still the northern terminus for the ferry running from Tobermory to Manitoulin Island. The boat at dock is the *S. S. Norisle*. Today's active ferry is the *M.V. Chi Cheemaun*, which means "big canoe" in the Ojibway language.

M.S. Chi-Cheemaun   *Aerial — Bryan H. Gleason*

No postmark. The *Chi Cheemaun* is the most recent ferry to run between South Bay Mouth on Manitoulin Island and Tobermory on the Bruce Peninsula. This ferry was built in Collingwood in 1974. It was operated originally by the Ontario Northland Co., but since 2002 it has been operated by the Owen Sound Transportation Co. The ferry is 365 feet long and is 6,990 gross tons. It can carry 638 passengers and 140 automobiles. During the height of the summer tourist season, it runs a regular schedule between South Bay Mouth and Tobermory.

No postmark. This postcard shows how the bow of the ferry opens up to facilitate loading of automobiles. The card appears to be a mate to the previous *M.S. ChiCheemaun* card.

JAWS   M.S. Chi-Cheemaun

Postmark is 1909. This is a serene view of the harbour of Pointe au Baril with its 1889 lighthouse. The lighthouse replaced an earlier pile of rocks with a lighted lantern on top of a barrel. The word "baril" is French for barrel.

At Point au Baril among the 30,000 Islands, Georgian Bay, Canada

Str. Majestic, Parry Sound

Postmark is 1902. The *Majestic*, built in 1895 at Collingwood for the Northern Navigation Line, ran from Collingwood to Sault Ste. Marie, Ontario, and made stops at the ports between. This card shows it entering Parry Sound harbour, which was considered to be one of the best natural harbours on the Great Lakes. The town was established in 1857 at the site of a sawmill. Named after Sir William Edward Parry, the Arctic explorer, by Henry Bayfield, who did the original survey of Georgian Bay. Built in 1889, *Majestic* opened the new Soo locks in the same year; it burned at Point Edward, Ontario, in 1915, and was a total loss. Parry Sound is also as the birthplace of Bobby Orr, the great NHL defense man.

No postmark. This photo of the Parry Sound Lumber Mill Ltd. was probably taken before 1910. The original lumber mill was situated at the mouth of the Sequin River and was built by the Beatty brothers.

Parry Sound Lumber Co's Mill, Parry Sound, Ont.

First Steam Boat Owned in Parry Sound, Tug Wave.

No postmark. The title is self-explanatory. I could not find much about this boat in my research. I suspect it was used in the lumber trade.

Postmark is 1909. This card shows three small boats in Parry Sound's natural harbour. They were probably used for transportation between the small communities along the east shore of Georgian Bay. At that time, boats like these served isolated lumber camps. A railway bridge in the background provided the only land link to the south, as there were no roads.

Rose Point Summer Resort, Parry Sound, Georgian Bay, Canada

Postmark is 1909. This photo shows the Rose Point Summer Resort which was one of the many summer hotels built by the railroads. The boat at the dock appears to be the *Emma*; it ran cruises in the Parry Sound area.

No postmark. This is a photo of the small steamer *Emma* at the Rose Point station dock. The *Emma* ran between Parry Sound and Depot Harbour. It sank in 1912, so the photo is before that date.

No postmark. This is a panoramic view of the CPR bridge and Parry Sound harbour.

No postmark. The printing on the card identifies the location. It was probably photographed before 1920. The boat could be the steamboat *City Of Toronto* arriving from its run from Penetanguishene. (Postcard has very poor print quality.)

Swing Bridge, near Rose Point, "30,000 Islands, Georgian Bay".—1

Scene from Hotel Belvedere, Parry Sound, Ontario, Canada

No postmark. This card shows a much larger passenger boat which could carry passengers throughout the Great Lakes. I could not identify it with certainty, but it could be the *Majestic* painted white. I am certain some readers of this volume will be able to identify it. The view is from the front of the old Belvedere Hotel on Belevedere Hill, which was still functioning as a hotel in 1949. It was built before 1890, so it had a long existence. Parry Sound's favourite son, Bobby Orr, worked there as a bell hop in high school.

The postmark is 1908. It shows the *Emma*, which ran between Parry Sound and Depot Harbour. Depot Harbour was established as the terminus on Georgian Bay for the Ottawa, Amprior and Parry Sound Railroad. In 1907, the CPR built a trestle to bridge the Sequin River. The CPR then took over the port. It was to be a major port receiving grain from Western Canada and the USA. Because of this new railway, a tourism boom began at the beginning of the 20th century, and many resorts were built in the area. When the CPR decided to construct their new facility near Victoria Harbour on Hogg's Bay [Port McNicoll] in 1911, Depot Harbour was abandoned and soon became a ghost town.

Grand Trunk Elevator, Depot Harbor, Parry Sound, Georgian Bay

At Honey Harbour, Georgian Bay District, Ont., Canada,
Grand Trunk Railway System

Postmark is 1913. This is an idyllic view of Honey Harbour. The card appears to be a commercial card published by the Grand Trunk Railway System which became a part of the CNR system around 1921.

Postmark is 1910. This another view of Honey Harbour. The vessel docked could be the steamer *John Lee*.

"The Royal" and Victoria House in Distance   Honey Harbor, Georgian Bay

No postmark. The title of the card is self-explanatory. The setting is perfect and somewhat idyllic. I wonder if this is not a postcard produced for a railway advertisement. Ordinarily the onlookers should be waving!

Steamer "John Lee" passing through Honey Harbour, Georgian Bay, Canada

No postmark. This view shows the *Midland City*, a day liner, which ran from Midland up through the 30,000 Islands to Parry Sound, with one of its stops being at Honey Harbour. She operated for 84 years. The *Midland City* was built in Scotland in 1874 and ended up being burnt and scuttled near the mouth of the Wye River to become part of a breakwater.

No postmark. The vessels pictured are wooden Fairmiles built in Canada for the World War II effort. Of the 80 Fairmiles built in Canada, 33 were built on the Great Lakes: eight in Penetanguishene, eight in Midland, eight in Sarnia, nine in Toronto and the rest in other parts of the country. They served as submarine chasers, minesweepers and rescue launches. In the Honey Harbour area, they were known as "Hornets for Hitler."

"Hornets for Hitler."

This resort was established by Nathan Nickerson in 1892. He and his brothers operated a saw mill on Hogg's Bay (Victoria Harbour). He and his son established this resort at Honey Harbour. In the 1920s, the Grisé family from Penetanguishene bought the resort and changed the name to Delawanna Inn. The Grisés owned the Royal Hotel across the small waterway from the Nickerson's Resort. The Delawanna Inn burnt twice, in 1952 and again in 1972, but each time the Grisé family quickly rebuilt.

Nickersons Cottage Resort, Honey Harbour, Georgian Bay, Canada.

Minnicoganashene, Georgian Bay

Postmark is 1908. This scene is very similar to the card below and appears to be have been taken from the same vantage point. Some of the same buildings are seen in both pictures. The dock where the *City of Dover* is tied up in the card below has not been built yet. This location is in the the 30,000 Islands, not too far from Honey Harbour. The spelling of Minicoganashene on the card has been modernized to "Minicognashene."

No postmark. It is a summer scene on Georgian Bay. The boat at the dock is probably the *City of Dover* out of Midland. There were scheduled trips all summer out of Midland running up to the cottage country, transporting passengers and their belongings. This photo probably was taken during the early part of the last century.

Minnicoganashene, Georgian Bay, Ont., Canada

In Freddie Channel, near Minnicoganashene, Georgian Bay

No postmark. The title of the card is self-explanatory. This location is also very close to where the other two photos were taken.

No postmark. The photo was taken among the 30,000 Islands on Georgian Bay. The *Sea Gull* was a small, nine-ton boat built at Port Severn in 1893. The other vessel is not identified.

CHAPTER 3

Southern Georgian Bay to Owen Sound

Waubaushene • Victoria Harbour • Port McNicoll • Midland • Penetenguishene
Collingwood • Thornbury • Meaford • Owen Sound

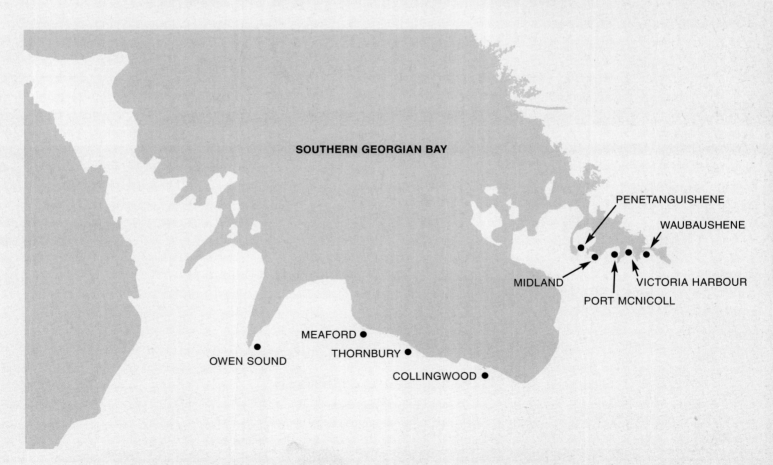

Postmark is 1938. The lumber mill appears to be quite active even at this late date for this part of Ontario. Extensive piles of cut lumber can be seen. Although the postmark is 1938, this photo could have been taken quite a bit earlier. Since the Phelps Dodge Co. owned this mill, they would have the resources to hire an "aeroplane" to take such a photo.

AN AEROPLANE VIEW OF WAUBAUSHENE, ONT.
PUBLISHED BY CANADIAN POST CARD CO. TORONTO.

Photo by G. A. Brown.

The Dock at Waubaushene, Ont.

No postmark. The dock as shown is probably the Phelps Dodge dock, where the yacht belonging to the Dodge family and a tug are moored. The tug was used to pull log booms across Georgian Bay to the American markets. Saginaw Bay would be one of the destinations. (Card is in very poor condition.)

A VIEW AT VICTORIA HARBOUR, ONT.

No postmark. Although the card is titled Victoria Harbour, the view is looking towards Port McNicoll. A black passenger boat is docked at the CPR slip. It is difficult to identify the vessel because all the CPR boats originally were painted black. The photo was probably taken before 1925. A more typical view of Victoria Harbour would be the lumber mills which existed prior to 1930.

No card.

Since I was born and raised in Port McNicoll, I think it would be appropriate to give this Bay Port a little more space in this volume. Although the village still exists, it is only a shadow of what it had been. At its prime, it was referred to as the "little Chicago of the north". The CPR establishment there has been totally abandoned. Everything has been razed: the freight sheds, flour sheds, round house, the station, administrative buildings, ice house, are all gone. There is one exception, and that is the grain elevator. To raze this huge, reinforced concrete structure would involve prohibitive costs and there would be environmental concerns. You just could not dump all this concrete and metal into the water. The materials would have to be trucked away. The grain elevator was at one time the second largest grain elevator in the world, after a grain elevator in Brazil. It was also known for the fastest grain unloading mechanism in the world. The elevator remains without its three moveable unloading legs, which have been dismantled and removed. Basically, the village is now a bedroom community for citizens who work elsewhere.

This sepia-toned postcard is the oldest card that I have of Port McNicoll. It shows the freight sheds still under construction. There is a tug on the other side of the floating work shed. The date would be about 1910 or 1911. (The card was badly damaged through rough handling.)

FREIGHT SHEDS AT PORT McNICOL, ONT.

No postmark. This boat is either the *Athabaska* or the *Alberta* at the freight shed dock in Port McNicoll. In the background is the bunkhouse built by the CPR to accommodate the longshoremen who worked on unloading the boats when docked with the bagged flour and grain from the the Lakehead, Chicago and Milwaukee. Judging by the number of houses, this photograph was taken quite early in the development of the community, probably before 1920.

A real photo of ships at Port McNicoll. Although the postmark is 1928, I believe this was taken about 1920. Of the two closer vessels, the one on the left is the *Finland*; the boat next to it is not identified. The writer of the message on the reverse has identified the left vessel in the background as the *Str. Hebard* (arrow head). This vessel obviously meant something to him. The vessel in the right foreground is either the *Alberta* or the *Athabasca*. The village of Port McNicoll has an unpaved main street. I can see the house our family lived in for many years and the CPR Inn which was finally torn down about 1965. Also identifiable is the Methodist Church which became the Roman Catholic Church in 1921.

The postmark is June 10, 1912. Port McNicoll officially opened May, 1912. The *Assiniboia* left on its first trip on May 4, 1912. All the CPR boats are shown at dock. The closest vessel is the *Keewatin*. Also note the elevator has only two unloading legs. The third one would be added later.

Post mark is 1915. This is only three years after Port McNicoll was founded. There are two unloading legs, and the grain elevator is only one third the size it would eventually become. Although the postmark is 1915, the actual event took place during 1912. The grainer is not identified.

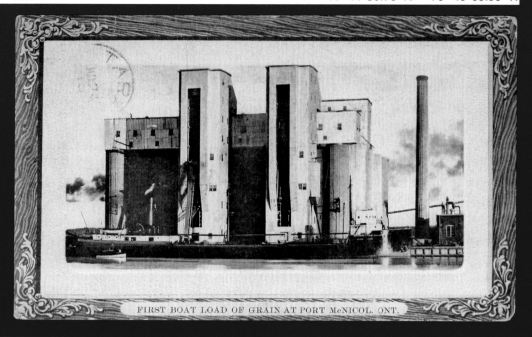

FIRST BOAT LOAD OF GRAIN AT PORT McNICOL. ONT.

Unloading an ice bound Freighter Port McNicoll

No postmark. This is an unusual card showing many workers with teams of horses cutting ice from around the ice-bound grain boat. This served two purposes: the ice, after being cut in blocks, could be stored in ice houses and then used on passenger trains for a primitive form of air conditioning. Also, removal of ice would allow the boat to move forward by winch power and allow another grainer behind it to move into a position to be unloaded. There are four boats docked behind the *W. Grant Morden*. This photo would be before 1920. My father worked for the CPR and in later years was involved in this type of work; it was very difficult, cold and dangerous.

No postmark. This photo is difficult to place; it could be early in the spring, with a grainer coming in to open the season. In the background are two of the CPR passenger boats at dock with no steam coming from their stacks. This makes me think that this is at the end of the shipping season and the grainer is coming to Port McNicoll for layup and unloading during the winter. Also, the ice on the water looks like late fall ice just starting to form.

No postmark. This photo shows the grain elevator at its original size, soon to increase three times, with another unloading leg added. The title on the card states the elevator is on "Maple Id." (Island) The island would soon become a peninsula. This photo was taken about 1913.

C.P.R. Elevator, Maple Id., Port McNichol, Canada   Constructed by John S. Metcalf Co., Chicago. Capacity, two million bushels.   Electric Motive Power

Photo by J.W.Bald

C. P. R.
Great Lakes Service
Port McNicoll.

Postmark is 1920. This CPR boat is black. The CPR passenger boats were painted white about 1920/21. The *Alberta* and *Athabasca* were never painted white, because they only did package freight to Chicago after World War I. This card is signed by the British artist G. F. Gillespie. After his signature, there is a number, 18, which is the year he painted this picture. He was hired by the CPR to do paintings not only of their lake boats, but also of their ocean liners and the CPR hotels across Canada, such as the Banff Springs Hotel in Alberta. (Print quality of the card is very poor.)

Card is on top of next page.

No postmark. Interesting real photo with four and possibly five boats at the elevator. To the right is a boat which is hard to identify, possibly the *Col. James M. Schoonmaker*. The three vessels to the left are the *Canadian Signaller*, the *Valcartier* and the *J.H. Sheadle*. The *Canadian Signaller* was built in 1919 at Collingwood as a "saltie". It was in the grain trade until 1925, when it was sold to James Playfair of Midland, who in turn sold it in a short time. It was then sold three more times, finally becoming part of the war effort in World War II, ending up in Great Britain. In 1941, it was lost at sea.

The *Valcartier* was built at Cleveland in 1903. In 1911 it rammed the steamer *John Mitchell* on Lake Superior. The *Mitchell* sank with the loss of three lives. It became the *Valcartier* when it was sold Canadian in 1914. During 1915, it was involved in another collision on Lake Huron and was heavily damaged. After five years, it was purchased by CSL and was a dependable income producer until it was scrapped in 1937.

The *J.H. Sheadle,* built in 1906, also has an interesting story, but we don't have the space to outline its history here. She survived the great storm of 1916, then was sold a few times and finally sold Canadian in 1979. During October 1979, she hit a shoal near Kingston, was declared unfit, and was sold for scrap to a company in Spain.

Since the *J.H. Sheadle* changed its name to *LaSalle* in 1928, and the *Canadian Signaller* was in the grain trade until 1925, it appears this photo was taken in the early 1920s.

See bottom of previous page for text.

C.P.R. Elevators   *Port McNicoll Ont*

C.P.R. Str "KEEWATIN"
PORT McNICOLL.

Postmark is 1924. The *Keewatin* is shown leaving Port McNicoll in the early 1920s. The flower gardens on the dock were later developed into a much visited, popular tourist attraction, especially after World War II. Not many passengers are on deck, which makes me believe the photo was taken after the busy summer season. The rear of the promenade deck is still open; later it was closed in to make a dance hall.

See card below

No postmark. The photo was taken between 1921 and 1922. This real photo shows the CSL grainer *Maplecourt* at the elevator. The elevator is now complete, with the last new section having been built and the third leg in place. The boat has a fascinating history. It began as the passenger vessel *Northwest* which, along with its sister ship the *Northland*, ran from Buffalo to Duluth. It was very expensive to run, but the owner, James J. Hill the railroad baron, kept the boat sailing because he thought it was good advertising for his railroad system out west. In 1911, the boat was damaged by a fire at dock in Buffalo. It was then cut in two to fit the St. Lawrence canal system at that time, and while being towed east on Lake Ontario for service during World War II, the bow section sank. The aft end was towed to Montreal and a new bow was added. It was virtually a new vessel and was named *Maplecourt* by its new owner,

the CSL company. The easily recognizable vessel was returned to the upper lakes service in 1922 and ran in the grain trade until 1929. In that year, she was wrecked on Cockburn Island in Georgian Bay. The boat was salvaged and became a salvage vessel for United Towing and Salvage Co. In 1940, the vessel was requisitioned by the Canadian Government for war service. On March 7, 1941, it was torpedoed by a U boat in the North Atlantic; there were no survivors.

See text above

One of the postcards provided by the CPR at every writing desk on board its three passenger boats. This photo is from about 1950. Note the well-kept flower gardens in the foreground, which were a favourite site for tourists to take photographs.

PORT MC NICOLL, ONTARIO

No postmark. The *Manitoba* is docked at the passenger dock at Port McNicoll. Not visible is the grand display of flower gardens and plants that eventually became a great attraction for tourists. This photo was taken out of season, probably prior to 1940.

This is a photo of the *Assiniboia* docked at the freight sheds at Port McNicoll. The card belongs to a set of Great Lakes postcards from the immediate post-World War II period. On the back of the card is this data: The *Assiniboia* was built in Govan, Scotland, in 1907. It was 336 feet long with a displacement of 3,880 tons. Her sister ship, the *Keewatin*, also crossed the Atlantic. Both ships were cut in half in Montreal to pass throught the small locks of the pre-Seaway canals and reassembled on fresh water. (Photo by Edward D. Clark.)

Another card from the series provided free for passengers of the CPR. Post-mark appears to be from 1951. The *Keewatin* seems to be ready to leave after embarkation of passengers from the boat train from Toronto.

No card

Originally known as Mundy's Bay during the 1830s, Midland was an agricultural village. In 1871, the first lumber mill was built with dock facilities. In 1879, Mundy's Bay became the terminus of the Midland Railway Corporation, which would connect Georgian Bay to Lake Ontario. This railway company built the first grain elevator. At the turn of the century, when lumber was still the primary industry, the Canada Iron Foundry was established. In 1910 the dry dock was built, followed in 1916 by the shipbuilding yard. During the 1920s, two more grain elevators were built. The shipyards were closed during the depression, but reopened during World War II for the war effort. They built Corvettes and Fairmiles. The ship yard strike of 1954 caused the company to close the yrd. Now, Midland has one grain elevator and several smaller industries. Tourism is probably its most important source of income today.

This card is postmarked 1905. The scene is of the dock area and marshalling yards of the Grand Trunk Railway. The GTR was started in 1905 in competition with the CPR. At one time, it had over 5,000 miles of track. It became over-extended and went bankrupt in 1919, when it was taken over by the Canadian government and eventually became the CNR.

No postmark. The photo shows part of the winter lay-up fleet in Midland Harbour. The locally known photographer J.W. Bald obviously could not get the whole fleet from from his vantage point on one of the freighters. Counting the smoke stacks, there are at least 12 boats in the picture.

Part of the Winter Fleet, Midland, Canada   Photo. by J. W. Bald

A Souvenir of Midland, Canada

The postmark is 1903. It is a real photo by J.W. Bald, showing the grain elevator built around 1880. The grainer is the *Rurlburt W. Smith* of U.S.T. Co. The boat unloading is not identified.

G. T. R. Elevator,   *Midland Esplanade, Can.*

Vertical card showing two G.T.R. elevators on top of each other. The image on the left is on the top. (The print quality of the card is very poor.)

This card is postmarked 1908. It shows two elevators belonging to the Grand Trunk Railway (G.T.R.) which was an independent railway competing with Canadian Pacific Railway (C.P.R.), but went into receivership and was taken over by the Canadian National Railway (C.N.R.). Both elevators have been demolished and replaced with upscale housing developments, naturally with a great water view!

Bottom photo on vertical card.

G.T.R. Tank Elevator, Midland, Can. Capacity 1,000,000 Bushels.

This card is postmarked 1908, but the photo was taken earlier during the construction of the elevator. The card shows the construction of the storage bins. The mouth of the Wye River is on the right.

Note: This old photograph shows a common problem encountered with silver halide photos as they age. The silver precipitates on the photo's surface, obliterating any photographic details. At the end of this irreversible process, no photo will be left.

Postmark is 1908. This is a view of the Tiffin grain elevator in Midland, the elevator located closest to the mouth of the Wye River. Midland at one time had four grain elevators, but the capacity of all four combined was less than that of the elevator at Port McNicoll. This elevator was demolished after the opening of the St. Lawrence Seaway, with the eventual transhipment of grain via Georgian Bay ports to Montreal having come to an end.

Post mark is 1908. This photo of the Aberdeen elevator is another card by J.W. Bald. The elevator was located between the Tiffin Elevator and the main town dock. The three grainers are riding high, their cargo of grain having been unloaded during winter. There is still ice on the bay, so I suspect this was early spring before the spring fit out.

Aberdeen Elevator, Midland, Canada   (Copyright).   Photo. by J. W. Bald

Postmark is 1909. This card shows the burning of Chew's mill. This mill competed with Playfair's mill. Fires of this type were common because of all the combustible wood lying around. Even though the chimneys of the furnaces used to burn sawdust and waste wood were quite high and were screened,but sparks still fell nearby or on the mill. During the height of the lumbering of white pine in Central Ontario, more mills were burned accidently than were torn down intentionally when they had outlived their usefulness.

Postmark is 1908. This is the Playfair Mill which Playfair bought from its founder; it became very succsessful. The photo was taken from the water side, showing the pikemen who directed and fed the logs into the mill for cutting into lumber.

"A Canadian Saw Mill"—Jas. Playfair's, Midland. Georgian Bay   Photo. by J. W. Bald

PLAYFAIR'S MILL WITH MILL IN DISTANCE, MIDLAND, ONT.

No postmark, but probably from about same time as the other picture of Playfairs mill, around 1910. This view is from inland and shows the cut lumber stacked on the ground, with some already loaded on flat cars ready to be shipped to the Eastern USA, or by ocean vessel to Great Britain.

Canada Iron Furnace Co's Plant, Midland

The postmark is 1906. This is a scene of the smelter which was owned by the Canada Iron Foundry. The dock appears to have timber stacks in the background, probably fuel for the blast furnaces.

No postmark. This card shows the massive furnaces of Canada Iron Corporation. The previous card is dated 1906, showing the Canada Iron Company Corporation, has two furnaces, while this card shows at least four furnaces. I suspect the date of this card to be 1909. The small vessel in the foreground is the *Voyageur*, a water bus, and the other appears to be a tug.

Furnaces of Canada Iron Corporation, Midland, Canada (capacity 450 tons daily)
Photo by J. W. Bald

No postmark. The title on the card is self-explanatory. This is probably the coal dock with coal for the the smelter nearby.

Docks & Unloading Equipment of the Great Lakes Transportation Co. Ltd., Midland, Can.

The postmark is 1916. This is the same photo as the Midland 4 card, but is presented differently. The photo is framed by imitation wood and the actual photo is tinted blue. It appears that the publisher decided to modernize the card and make it more attractive for sale. The first card was postmarked 1903. The publisher decided to get more mileage out of the older photo and save some money.

A Souvenir of Midland, Canada

Souvenir of MIDLAND

No postmark. This card shows the main town dock. In the foreground is the delivery boat that was used by Preston's grocery store to deliver groceries and supplies to the cottagers that were scattered throughout the 30,000 Islands. In the background is the Townhouse grain elevator. This was probably the last elevator to be built about 1918.

THE HARBOR, MIDLAND, ONT.

THE HARBOR, MIDLAND, ONT.

No post mark. This is an early scene of Midland harbour. Card was made in Germany but published in Midland. The grainer is not identifiable. The photo was probably taken before World War II.

No postmark. It appears that the peripatetic photographer J.W. Bald photographed this scene during the early spring, prior to Spring fit out. The steamers do not have any smoke coming from their stacks and there appears to be some ice on the bay. All three boats have been lightened, probably during the winter. Also interesting is that the two boats in the right background appear to be whalebacks. The Simcoe elevator was demolished a few years ago, with a cost overrun because of the massive reinforced concrete constration. It is now the site of a large marina.

No postmark. It appears that the "docks" were recently completed and the photographer J.W. Bald made note of this on the card. The large vessel is the *S.S. Noronic.* The *Noronic* was launched at Port Arthur in 1913.

See photo below

No postmark. This is an unusual photograph by J.W. Bald of Midland, Ontario. It shows three of the most popular Great Lakes passenger boats docked together at Midland. In the middle is the tragic *Noronic,* which burned at dock in Toronto in 1949. More about this boat is written elsewhere in this volume. The *South American* and the *North American* were built at Ecorse Michigan; the *North American* in 1913 and the *South American* in 1914. The *South American* was about 345 gross tons heavier than its sister ship. The *South American* was to sail between Chicago and Duluth, while the *North American* was to sail between Chicago and Buffalo. After the opening of the St. Lawrence Seaway, the *South American* often included Montreal in its itinerary. It carried over a half a million passengers between the ports of Chicago, Detroit, Duluth and Buffalo over a career than spanned 50 years. The *North American finally* retired in

1964 and was sold to the Seafarers Union to be used at their School for Seamanship at Piney Point, Md. as a floating barracks for the students. It sunk off Nantucket Massachusetts in 1967 while being towed to Piney Point, Maryland.

In the same year, the union bought the *South American* for the same purpose, but this had to be abandoned because of new safety laws passed by congress in regards to fire hazards on ships with wooden super structures. The *South American* was moved to Camden, New Jersey, where it deteriorated at dock and finally was broken up at Baltimore in 1992.

See text above.

The *North American*, *Noronic* and the *South American* at the Midland dock.

Copelands Mill and Great Lake Transportation Cos Elevator and Dryer, Midland, Ont., Can.

The postmark is 1931. This shows the grain elevator and dryer of the Great Lakes Transportation Company. The Copelands Flour Mill on the left has now been built.

Postmark is 1938. This real photo of the *S.S. Noronic* shows it approaching the Town Dock in Midland. A glimpse of the Simcoe elevator in the distance shows a lightened grainer docked nearby, probably "mothballed." World War II had not yet started and the Great Depression was just over. At that time, many lake boats were inactive. After docking, one of the side trips offered to the passengers by the *Noronic* was a trip to the Martyrs' Shrine and the site of the martyrdom of the 17th century Jesuit Saints, Brébeuf and Lalemant.

NORONIC AT MIDLAND

The postmark is 1943. The autos in the photo are pre-World War II models. The *South American* is docked. This is a real photograph by J.W. Bald. Three grainers docked in the background appear to be laid up; that situation would soon change.

"Midland Harbor"

NORONIC - MIDLAND ELEVATOR

The postmark is 1947. This view shows the *S.S Noronic* entering Midland harbor with the Simcoe Elevator in the background. This elevator has been demolished and has been replaced by a marina for pleasure craft. The card was mailed two years before the *Noronic* burnt in Toronto harbour during September 1949, with a great loss of life.

Postmark is 1946. The following description of the *Midland City* taken from the publication *Shipwrecks of Southeastern Georgian Bay* gives a good summary:

"The *Midland City* was a familiar passenger steamer during the 1900s. She was built in Scotland in 1871 and operated for 84 years. Beginning in 1921, she made daily runs between Midland and Parry Sound. In 1933, her steam engines were replaced with a diesel motor. As cars became popular, her daily trips became less necessary. In 1955, she was towed to the Wye river, dismantled and burned. The remains of the *Midland City* are now part of the breakwall located at Wye Heritage Marina.

No postmark. This view shows the *Midland City* getting some reconditioning work done on its hull. In 1955 it was dismantled and sunk, so the photo is before 1955.

"S.S. Georgian" Midland harbor.

Postmark is 1947. The *Rochester* was built in 1910 at Wyandotte, Michigan. She had 120 state rooms and 16 parlours and ran trips on Lake Ontario. In 1915, she sailed on Lake Michigan. A lawsuit kept her in lay-up until 1917. She was sold to the Northern Navigation Division of the CSL and sailed on Georgian Bay. In 1919, her name was changed to *Cape Eternity* and she sailed on the Saguenay route until 1925. She was laid up at Toronto during the Great Depression. In 1935, she was rebuilt and ran between Windsor and Georgian Bay. In World War II, was a floating barracks for the Canadian Navy. In 1946, she was sold to a Chinese company and renamed *Ha Sin*. After the Chinese communist revolution, she was broken up for scrap.

No postmark. This is a panoramic view of Penetanguishene which was a bustling Bay Port at one time. Etienne Brulé was the first European to visit this site between 1610 and 1614. He had been sent by Champlain to live among the native Hurons to learn their language and make friends with them. In 1793, Lord Simcoe visited this harbor and recommended that Britain purchase it from the natives because it was an ideal harbor and would be easy to defend in case of a naval attack. The naval base was established here in 1817. At the beginning of the 20th century, there was an active lumber industry. Now it is mainly a tourist destination featuring the historic site of "Discovery Harbour."

Water Front, Penetanguishene, Canada.

Postmark is 1900. Regattas were very popular entertainments during the early part of the 20th century in many of the harbours on the Great Lakes. Spectators are dressed quite formally with ladies in showy dresses and the men in suits.

Postmark is 1900. This is the dock at the Penetanguishene Hotel. The photo appears to have been taken about the same time as the "regatta" card above. It appears that the steamer seen in the "regatta" card has just docked and is taking on passengers.

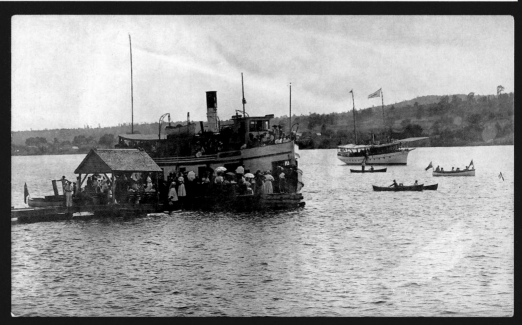

No postmark. This card shows the *Waubic* at the dock at Penetanguishene. At this time, it may not have been part of the Northern Navigation Line. The boat closest to it is the *Electric*. Also note the team of horses in front of a carriage or wagon. The photographer was the peripatetic J.W. Bald of Midland, Ontario.

Str. City of Toronto, Penetanguishene to Parry Sound.

Postmark is 1909. This photo shows the *City of Toronto*, a sidewheeler, heading out of Penetanguishene harbour during one of its regular runs to Parry Sound. It also would call at Collingwood and Midland. Its construction was similar to that of the *S.S. Waubuno*, which ended up a tragic loss.

No postmark. This sepia-tinted card shows the steamer *Waubic*, which ran from Penetang to Midland and Parry Sound, arriving at the pier in Penetanguishene. It sailed for the Northern Navigation Line. The boat was built at the Collingwood Shipyards in 1909; it was tranferred to Lake Erie and burned at the dock at Kingsville in 1938. It was rebuilt and sold to Nova Scotia owners and burned again in 1959, this time a total loss.

No postmark. Similar to the previous photo. and possibly taken at the same time. Note the woman in the white dress! Photo probably was taken in the late 1920s or early 1930s, prior to 1938.

Str. "Waubic" Penetang to Parry Sound—Photo by J. W. Bald.

No postmark. Str. *Waubic* again, but this time among the 30,000 Islands. Photo is a copy of a postcard by J.W. Bald of Midland, locally famous for his postcard views of Georgian Bay.

Postmark is 1946. This card shows the S.S. *South American* approaching the dock at Penetanguishene. Penetanguishene and Midland were regular ports of call for the *South American* and its sister ship, the *S.S North American* during July and August. The *South American* was the last passenger boat to do cruises on the Great Lakes, until the recent invasion by smaller, foreign cruise ships that split their schedule between the Great Lakes during the summer and the Caribbean during the winter.

S.S. South American in Harbour, Penetanguishene, Ontario. 4

The Harbor, Collingwood

Postmark is 1900. This is a panoramic view of Collingwood harbour, taken with the photographer standing most likely in front of the grain elevator in the card below. There are about nine smoke stacks. The way the boats are docked, with no smoke coming from the stacks, means that this is a pre-season view.

No postmark. The photo was probably taken between 1900 and 1910, when a lot of similar views were seen in postcards of harbour scenes. It appears to be late in winter, with ice still around. One smokestack is belching smoke, leading me to assume that this was the time when the crews arrived at their boats prior to spring outfitting.

The Docks, Collingwood, Ont., Canada.

This is a photograph by E.S. Brown, photographer in Collingwood but published in Toronto. It is probably early spring time, with no smoke coming from the stacks.

Collingwood was incorporated as a town in 1858. It was named after Admiral Collingwood, second in command to Lord Nelson at the battle of Trafalgar. It was an important rail terminus for shipping to and from the Lakehead. The trains would bring products from Toronto, Montreal and other eastern cities. The shipyards were built in 1883. After the closing of the shipyards and the decline in the grain trade, Collingwood continued to prosper as a popular tourist destination for boating and skiing.

THE HARBOR   COLLINGWOOD, ONT.

E. S. Brown, Collingwood   1673

In the Harbor, Collingwood, Canada.

No postmark. Another scene in the harbour, but now two boats have steamed up and are either arriving or leaving. The closer boat in the right foreground appears to be a side paddle wheeler.

The postmark is 1906. This is a nice sepia photo of a steamer (grain boat/iron ore carrier) ready for launching. The writing on the card states that the launching is scheduled for the afternoon of December 5. This appears to be a pre-launch photo to be sold to the attendees, or as a gift for the invited guests.

The postmark is unclear, but appears to be 1906. The steamer is ready for launching, with all the dignitaries in place.

LAUNCHING OF STEAMER "COLLINGWOOD"   COLLINGWOOD, CANADA

Published for E. S. Brown, Collingwood 4968

The postmark is 1908. The photo shows the launching of the steamer *Collingwood* just after removal of the wooden blocks. The photographer is a E. S. Brown of Collingwood. This launching took place on October 5, 1907. The *Collingwood* remained in the grain trade for many years. During August 1909, she was rammed and sunk in the Detroit River. She was raised and in 1918 sold to the C.S.L. In 1950, she was converted to a package freighter. In 1968 at age 61, she was sold for scrap and towed to Spain .

The postmark is 1948. This is an unusual card illustrating a boat in dry dock, probably for repairs, an overhaul, or just for inspection of the hull.

DRY DOCK, COLLINGWOOD

Largest passenger steamer in Canada, "Hamonic" built at Collingwood, Ont., launched 26th Nov. 1908, 365 feet over all, 6200 horse power, freight capacity 3000 tons.

This card is self-explanatory, with all the important information on its face. Interestingly enough, the card was published by a Dr. E.L. Connolly of Collingwood.

Postmark is 1909. Another scene of the harbour at Collingwood, with eight boats docked and no smoke coming from the stacks in this view. Again, it is probably in the early spring. The card's publisher is different from the previous two cards, so the photographer is probably different.

The Harbour, Collingwood, Canada

Postmark is 1911. View of the main dock area at that time. Fourteen stacks can be counted. This makes me believe that this view was taken in spring, before the sailing season opened up.

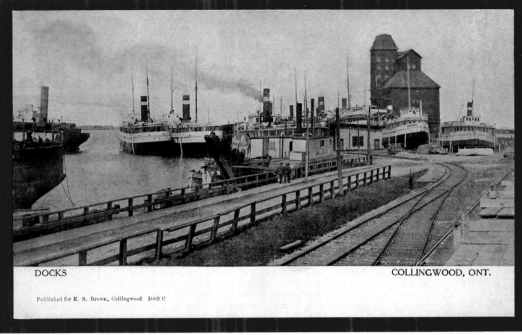

DOCKS   COLLINGWOOD, ONT.

Published for E. S. Brown, Collingwood 1069 C

No postmark, but the card is probably from the late 1930s or early 1940s. Seen docked side by side is the *Alfred Krupp*, registered in Montreal, which could be a barge, and the *John A. Halloway*. Notice the lack of boat activity in the harbour at this time, compared to the early part of the century.

The Harbour and Elevators, Collingwood, Ontario, Canada.—1.

This view is of the *Montclair* being launched in 1956. The postmark is 1959. She appears to be a ship for ocean cargo.

Postmark is 1907. The village of Thornbury was first settled by a man from Ottawa. He built a flour mill on the Beaver River. Early on, the village was simply called Beaver River, but later it got the name Thornbury, probably after a town in England. At the time of this card, it was a very busy community with a boat dock, three mills, and four hotels. The port would be a regular stop for the small passenger/freight boats that sailed on Georgian Bay. The so called "typical Canadian girl" would enhance the card and help to to sell it.

The Harbour, Georgian Bay, Meaford, Ont.

No postmark. This harbour scene of Meaford reveals only a yacht at dock. The card was probably produced in the 1920s. The card does'nt do justice to the town because much larger boats called there, especially before 1913 when the grain elevator burnt down. The Grand Trunk Railway made Meaford a terminal in 1901. After the fire, Meaford lost its importance as a Bay Port for transhipment of grain from to Lakehead to southern Ontario. The village was given its name in 1845.

Postmarked 1906. The photo on this card was taken at least 6 years before the elevator burned. Meaford was quite a bustling Bay Port. To the left is a steam dredge hard at work, accompanied by a tug. The boat unloading at the elevator flies the American Flag,

Meaford Harbour

How do you like it? I wasn't sure of your name. Please excuse the ink on this. I'm in a hurry.

HARBOR

OWEN SOUND, ONT.

Warwick Bro's & Rutter, Limited Publishers, Toronto   1555

Postmark is 1905. Probably taken in early spring before the opening of the sailing season, because all five CPR boats are at dock. Note how the harbour narrows. This was one of the reasons the CPR decided to abandon Owen Sound in 1911. The larger two boats, *Keewatin* and *Assiniboia*, had to back up before they could turn around. The other reason CPR left was the railroad grade out of Owen Sound at 2.3 degrees. The CPR spent a lot of money reducing the grade to 1.0 degree. Boxcars loaded with grain had to be marshalled out of Owen Sound before they could be taken to Montreal. A "convenient" fire burned down the grain elevator in 1911.

No postmark. This appears to be another layup scene in Owen Sound harbour. The CPR freight shed, the grain elevator and at least one passenger boat are in the photo. The elevator burnt in 1911, so this photo was taken before that date.

Owen Sound Harbor looking North

102,837.

No postmark. Another scene in Owen Sound harbour with at least eight boats visible and some "double parked." Makes me think that this is lay up in late Fall or fitting out during spring.

No postmark. A closeup view of the narrowest part of the Sydenham River, showing how crowded the harbour at Owen Sound became during the winter lay ups. Parts of eleven vessels are visible in the photo. Also interesting is the boat that appears to have sunk at the dock, and the two men looking the situation over.

No postmark. This photo, which was taken about 1905, demonstrates how narrow the Owen Sound harbour is, making it hard for the CPR boats *Keewatin* and *Assiniboia* to turn around. The closer vessel is the *Keewatin* or *Assiniboia*, while the other boat would be the *Alberta* or *Athabaska*.

The Harbour, Owen Sound, Ont., Canada

OWEN SOUND   HARBOR IN WINTER.

No postmark. View is taken from the deck of a boat, apparently in the middle of winter. The CPR boats appear to be in the left background. This again would help to date the photo before 1911. A smoke stack count indicates about twelve boats laid up in the harbour.

Harbor, Owen Sound, Canada.

Postmark is 1910. This view looks down the Sydenham River towards Georgian Bay. The black vessel on the right is probably one of the CPR boats, the *Alberta* or the *Athabaska*. The closer vessel on the right I cannot identify with certainty. In the left foreground is a tug which was very useful in this narrow harbour.

No postmark. Another view of Owen Sound harbour, again with idled boats. It appears the photographers competed to see who could get the most vessels in a scene! My count is about fourteen boats. Again, the view is probably before the Spring fit up. This view also shows how narrow the harbour at Owen Sound was.

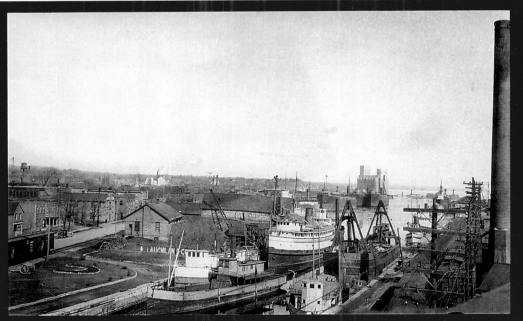

The Harbour, Owen Sound, Ont., Canada

106.592.

No postmark. A partial view of twelve boats. This photograph was taken in early spring before fit out, probably in 1911. Three of the boats in the right background are probably CPR boats. The closest boat on the right is the *Caribou*, built at Goderich, Ontario, in 1904 for the Dominion Transportation Company. It was in use by the Owen Sound Transportation Company from 1904 until 1946 as a North Channel passenger boat and freighter travelling from Owen Sound to the Soo. From 1945, it was used as a ferry along with the *Normac* on the Tobermory to South Bay Mouth run. In 1947, the *Norisle* replaced the *Caribou*, which was then rebuilt as a floating hotel; this venture was soon abandoned

No postmark. This is a picture of the *Alberta* at the CPR freight shed in Owen Sound harbour. Because the CPR moved to their new home port of Port McNicoll in 1911/12, this photo was taken before then.

No postmark. A grain boat of the 1920s, probably the *Newt Smith*, is unloading at the grain elevator which has a single leg. Note the open framework on the left of the elevator, which means it was still undergoing some form of construction.

No postmark. The small steamboat is the *S.S. Telegram*, operated by the Owen Sound Transportation Company as a ferry from the Canadian Lake Erie mainland to Pelee Island. The photo was taken between 1909 to 1913. Many boats were used as ferries to Pelee Island, but since it was only a seven month season, the route was never very profitable. The dock is probably at Owen Sound.

No postmark. This photo shows the *Noronic*, with all flags flying and decks packed with passengers, apparently turning in Owen Sound harbour. The automobiles on the dock appear to be from the early 1920s (also note there are no horse carriages). One can see the bulging on the sides of the boat. After launching, she flipped over from being top-heavy. Part of the solution was to produce bulging bulkheads on both sides, low down at and below water level, which were filled with concrete.

No postmark. This is a rare postcard showing the *S.S. Keewatin* at dock in Owen Sound, with its decks lined with passengers at what seems to be a festive occasion. I believe this was a "day" excursion from Port McNicoll. A study of the automobiles on the dock suggests that the photo was taken during the early 1930s. The closest car appears to be a 1930/1932 Dodge. Also seen is a late 1920s Ford. The two automobiles closest to the freight shed appear to be 1933 models, because that was the year manufacturers introduced the distinctive trunks.

MANITOBA.   OWEN SOUND.

No postmark. Real photo of the *S.S. Manitoba*. Few passengers are aboard, so this photo was not taken during July and August, the peak season. The *Manitoba* continued to make Owen Sound part of its scheduled stops after the CPR moved to their new port on Hogg's Bay. Apparently, the CPR did not want to lose "docking rights." Also during the *Manitoba's* lay over in Port McNicoll, after returning from its weekly trip to the Lakehead, she would do day excursions to Owen Sound. After the burning of the *S.S. Noronic* in Toronto in September 1949, all passenger boats had to comply with new and expensive safety regulations. Many of the aging boats on the Great Lakes were scrapped, since it was not cost effective to update them.

The postmark is 1941. This photo shows the *S.S. North American* arriving in Owen Sound harbour. To the right is the boat *S.S. Manitoulin*. In 1841, Owen Sound was called Sydenham after the river it is located on. It was renamed Owen Sound in 1851. From 1885 to 1911, the town advertised itself as "The Gateway to the West." Many Canadians know Owen Sound as the birthplace of the World War II fighter plane Ace Billy Bishop. The CPR selected Owen Sound as the southern terminus of their lake service in 1883, using chartered vessels. Then they ordered three boats from a shipyard in Scotland: the *Algoma*, the *Alberta* and the *Athabaska*.

The Harbour, Owen Sound, Ontario.—26

S.S. North and South American in Harbour, Owen Sound, Ontario. —23.

N o postmark. Unusual photo showing both the *South American* and the *North American* at dock together in Owen Sound. This is a card from the late 1930s or early 1940s.

P ostmark is 1958. This photo of the *Norgoma* was taken in 1956 or 1957 (see truck). The *Norgoma* ran a schedule between Owen Sound and Sault Ste. Marie via the North Channel and made several stops in between.

CHAPTER 4

Wiarton, Tobermory and Lake Huron

Wiarton • Tobermory • Port Elgin • Kincardine • Goderich
Point Edward • Sarnia

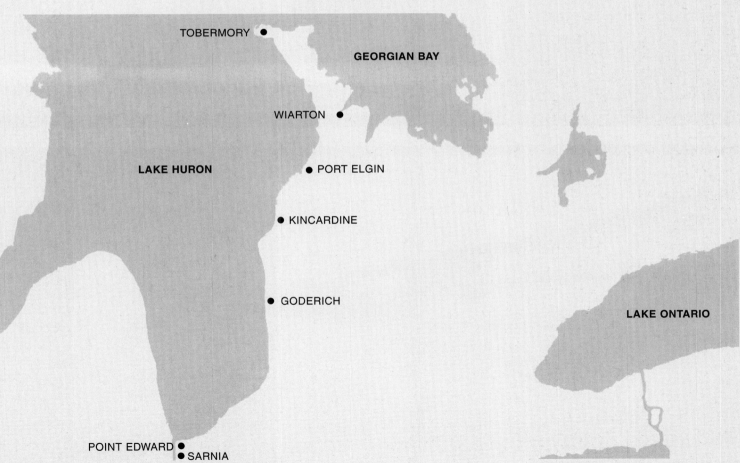

TOBERMORY

GEORGIAN BAY

WIARTON

LAKE HURON

PORT ELGIN

KINCARDINE

GODERICH

LAKE ONTARIO

POINT EDWARD
SARNIA

Wiarton was founded during the mid 1850s; it is named after the place in England where the Governor General of Canada at that time was born. It was an early landing area and portage point for Indians and voyageurs to cross over to Lake Huron. This is the narrowest point of the Bruce Peninsula. In its hay day, Wiarton had seven lumber mills. Today, it is a summer tourist destination. The card shows the steamer *Collingwood* entering Wiarton harbour with a full load of passengers. It appears to be a typical weekend excursion.

Str. Collingwood, Wiarton, Ont.

B. 389.   The Cliffs, Wiarton, Ont.

Postmark is 1929. The photo shows the fish house beneath the "Cliffs," established by the Buffalo Fish Co. in 1883. The company was very successful and, by 1891, was the largest fishing operation in Ontario. In the winter, ice would be cut on Colpoy's Bay for freezing fish for transport to the large eastern cities. In 1898, the Booth Fish Co. of Chicago took over. By 1932, the eel infestation reached Lake Huron and attacked the lake trout; this, combined with the depression, caused the Booth Co. to close operations. In 1935, a local owner took over and the fish house continued to operate until 1966, when it was permanently closed. The Wiarton Marina now occupies the site.

Tobermory, Georgian Bay.

Am sorry I can't more space.

Postmark is 1909. At the dock is a two-masted schooner; to the right, a small steam tug is underway.

No postmark. The steamer *Meaford* is shown approaching Tobermory. This area was first surveyed by British Admiral William Fitzwilliam Owen. The survey was completed by better-known Lt. Henry Bayfield in 1818. Tobermory was first called Collins Harbour, but the name was changed to Tobermory by Scottish settlers who came here from Goderich to fish. They named it after their home town in Scotland. These settlers established many fishing stations in the area. Almost at the same time, the lumber industry was developing, and by 1900 there were three large saw mills in the area.

Str. Meaford at Tobermory

The Normac at Tobermory, Ont., Canada.   48

No postmark, but date written on reverse is 1943. The *Normac* was built in Port Huron in 1902, originally as a fire tug. It was purchased by the Owen Sound Transportation Co. and, in 1932, was converted to carry automobiles, freight and passengers. It was 124 feet long and had a gross tonnage of 462 tons. The *Normac* ran on the Tobermory to South Bay Mouth route as a "ferry" until 1962. It was sold and was then converted to a "floating restaurant," but it did not "float" long at its dock in Toronto; it sank at the dock.
(Print quality of print is very poor.)

Although there is no postmark, this photo of the *S.S. Norisle* at dock was taken most likely during the early 1950s. This boat ran on a regular schedule from Owen Sound to Sault Ste. Marie, with stops at Tobermory, Little Current and other harbours.

Norisle at the Dock, Tobermory, Ontario, Canada,—11.

Postmark is 1907. Scene of Port Elgin, which is situated on a natural harbour directly west of Owen sound on Lake Huron. It was settled during the mid 1800s and became a busy lake port. After 1900, it declined in importance and is now a tourist port for small recreational boats. There has been an increase in population in the last 50 years because of the nearby Bruce Nuclear facility. The second boat in the photo is the tug *R.H. Dobson* which, in 1936, was involved near the North Shore in the rescue of two members of the crew of the fishing boat *EPM Purvis*. The *EPM Purvis* had an explosion on board and sank.
(Quality of photo and print is very poor.)

Port Elgin Harbor

On the Beach at Kincardine, Ont.

No postmark. Self-explanatory card. Long pier on the right, with no boats visible. I wonder if this is late Fall? The first settlers arrived in Kincardine on Lake Huron in 1848. The area was called "Penetangore," which is Indian for a "river with sand on one side." (Compare to Penetanguishene on Georgian Bay, "the place of white rolling sands.") The area was named Kincardine in 1857. Early on, there was a distillery and a brewery. Later, a substantial fishing industry developed which was ended by the invasion of the lamprey eel.

No postmark. Two CSL boats are docked. The CSL started in 1845 as a river boat line on the St. Lawrence. The company built its first self-unloader on the Great Lakes in 1924. These vessels were short enough to traverse the Lachine Canal and Lock system. In 1926, the CSL purchased the James B. Playfair Line of the Glen boats and gave the CSL a real presence on the upper Great Lakes. The photo is probably from the late 1920s. Goderich, founded in 1827, was named after Viscount Goderich, who was Prime Minister of England in 1827 and resigned in 1828. Walt Disney's father was born on a farm outside of Goderich and later emigrated to the USA. Walt was born in Chicago, Illinois.

The Harbour, Goderich, Ontario.

In Winter Quarters, Goderich, Ont.

No postmark. Four boats are in winter lay up at Goderich. The photo was probably taken in the spring, just as the ice was breaking up. The closest boat is the *Renvoyle*. This could be the former *Glenledi* which was renamed in 1926. The *Renvoyle* sunk after a collision at Point Edward on the St. Clair river in 1967; it was eventually sold for scrap. (Card has extremely poor print quality.)

A Fleet of Grain Vessels, representing Two Million Dollars, in Winter Quarters, Goderich Harbour, Ont., Canada

Postmark is not clear. This is another winter view of Goderich. There are four boats at dock but none is identifiable. One boat has the CSL colours on the stack. One elevator has the name Purity Flour written on it; this company was formed in 1917, thus this photo had to be taken after 1917! I obtained this card from the daughter of Captain James Foote of Collingwood; he had sent it to his wife back in Collingwood from Goderich while his grain boat was unloading at an elevator there. His daughter was married to Bob Portland from Collingwood, who played hockey for the old NHL team, the New York Americans, in the late 1930s.

No postmark. This is a panoramic view of the Maitland River and the long pier. It is an unusual view because no vessels are visible.

River and Harbor, Goderich.

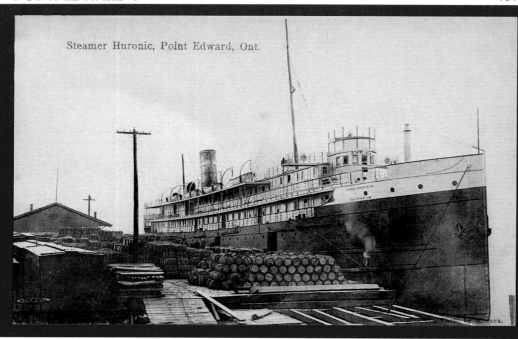

Steamer Huronic, Point Edward, Ont.

No postmark. Photo shows the *Huronic* at dock in Point Edward. The *Huronic* belonged to the Northern Navi-gation Co. out of Sarnia. At the time this photo was taken, this shipping line was affiliated with the Grand Trunk Railway. The Grand Trunk Railway became part of the CNR System about 1920. Point Ed-ward is the community on the Canadian side of the Blue Water Bridge located on the shore of the St. Clair River. The village was established in 1878.

No postmark. Title of card is self-explanatory. Port Huron is visible across the St. Clair River. This card is probably from the early 1940s.

Blue Water International Bridge over St. Clair River at Point Edward, near Sarnia, Ontario Canada. —31.

Postmark is 1906. This card is by Mc-crae & Co. Several small vessels are docked. The boat which appears to be leaving the dock is probably the *Huronic*. A tug seems to be assisting its departure. Note the stacked lumber on the dock.

Postmark 1906. Therefore this scene along along the docks of Sarnia was closer to 1900. Boats are not identified. The passenger boat (possibly the *Owana*) is probably a day liner or ferry that plied the St.Clair River and its confines. Note the piles of lumber, again testifying to the importance of the lumber trade at the turn of the century. There are no grainers. In 1836, Port Sarnia was established. Twenty years later it was incorporated as the City of Sarnia. A railroad tunnel was dug under the St. Clair River in 1889, connecting Sarnia with the USA. In 1938, the Bluewater Bridge was opened.

No postmark. The photo probably was taken around 1906. Unusual view showing a log boom with five tugs working to handle the boom. The card is titled "Five million feet. Sixty two thousand logs in one raft". I wonder who counted them! Rafts of this size were often pushed across Georgian Bay and Lake Huron from northern Georgian Bay and the Muskoka District to American harbours, especially Saginaw Bay. This is another McCrae card.

Postcard is dated 1911. This is a view of the Northern Navigation Line dock. In the background, a loaded grain boat is entering the harbour.

4574. Boats on River Front, Sarnia, Ont.

Postmark is 1912. This photo shows boats lined up on the river front. There appear to be ten vessels docked. The closest one is the *Saronic*. The fourth boat in line appears to be the passenger boat *Huronic*. There is evidence of ice on the river, so the photo probably was taken in Spring, prior to the opening up of the shipping season .

No postmark. This is obviously an advertising postcard for Macdonald Engineering Company of Canada, who built the grain elevator. The grain boat at dock is the *C.W. Watson*.

1,000,000 BUSHEL STORAGE AND CAR SHIPPING ELEVATOR WITH 25,000 BUSHEL PER HOUR VESSEL UNLOADING LEG DESIGNED AND BUILT FOR SARNIA ELEVATOR CO., LTD. SARNIA, ONTARIO

MACDONALD ENGINEERING CO. OF CANADA, LTD. 1102 C. P. R. BLDG., TORONTO MACDONALD ENGINEERING CO. SAN FRANCISCO   CHICAGO   NEW YORK

No postmark. This view shows the *Noronic* to the left. Careful observation again shows the previously noted bulging of the sides of the *Noronic*. Because there a no passengers on the *Noronic's* deck, but people ashore in front of the buildings, could mean that this view was shot just before embarkation of passengers for the boat's weekly cruise. The *Owana* is also at dock; it was a dayliner and ferry.

Postmark is 1947. This real photo card shows the ill-fated *S.S. Noronic* passing under the Blue Water Bridge connecting Port Huron, Michigan with Sarnia, Ontario; the actual Canadian end of the bridge is at Point Edward. The bridge was opened in 1938 and later, after much use, was totally refurbished.

CHAPTER 5

Lake St. Clair and Lake Erie

**Wallaceburg • Walkerville • Windsor • Chatham • Erieau • Port Stanley
Port Burwell • Port Dover • Port Colborne • Crystal Beach**

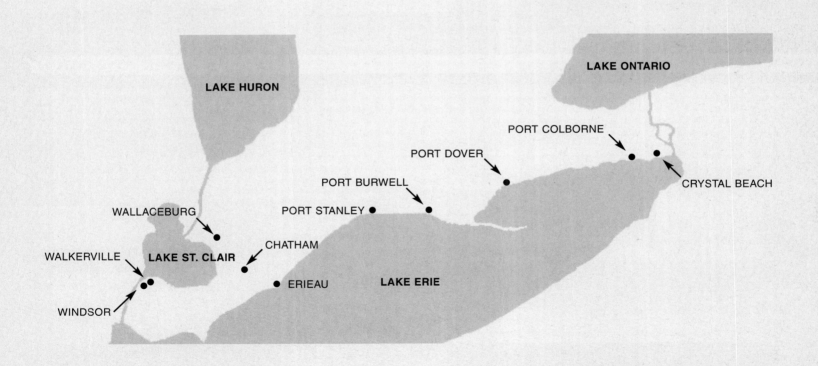

Postmark is 1906. This card shows the dock area on the Sydenham river with four boats; two with smokestacks indicating engine power, and two schooners. Cargo probably would be board lumber or grain. Wallaceburg is only 90 miles (144Km) from Detroit. Today, Wallaceburg has diversified industries, calling itself "The Tool and Die Capital of North America." There was no commercial shipping in or out of Wallaceburg from 1987 to 2003. Planned for 2003 was the delivery of 60,000 tons of gravel by barge and tug.

River Scene, Wallaceburg, Ont.

Steamer "Claremont" at the Do. Sugar Co. plant, Wallaceburg, Ontario.

No postmark. The steamer at dock was the third purchase of the Misener fleet in 1923. Built in Toledo Ohio, she started off as the *Erwin L. Fisher*. A self-unloader, she was destined for the lumber trade. During World War I, she sailed on the Atlantic for the French government. On return to the USA, she operated on the East Coast as the *Bayersher*. In 1922, she returned to the Great Lakes as the *Claremont*. At the end 1929, she returned to USA registry, was renamed and converted to a sand sucker. On July 19, 1930, she capsized and sank off Dunkirk, N.Y. with the loss of all 16 crewmen.

The card shows the boat docked at the Dominion Sugar Co. plant, which operated in Canada from 1925 to 1931.

120

No postmark, but published before 1907. This card shows a steamer at the passenger pier at Walkerville. The community was started by Hiriam Walker of distillery fame. Incorporated as a town in 1890, it was a true "company town" run by the Walker family, who were respected and considered very benevolent, providing free fire protection, free police service, street lighting and running water. Walkerville is now a suburb of Windsor. The boat appears to be a steamer serving communities along the Detroit River. I am sure the local historians will be able to identify it.

Postmark is 1908. This is a view of the ferry dock at Ferry Landing at Windsor. It appears the ferry boat has just arrived and passengers are disembarking. No vehicles on site, not even a horse-drawn carriage. Detroit is not visible in the background.

FERRY LANDING, WINDSOR ONT.

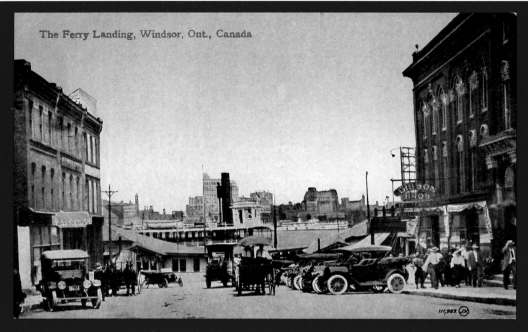

The Ferry Landing, Windsor, Ont., Canada

No postmark. Same view of the Ferry Landing as the previous card, but with two horse-drawn conveyances and several early vintage autos in the picture. Thus, the photo was taken several years after the other photo, probably in 1919 or in the early 1920s.

Postmark is 1913. This card shows the *Pere Marquette* at the ferry dock in Windsor. The ferries transported railway cars from Windsor to Detroit and back.

Pere Marquette Slip Dock, Windsor, Canada.

No postmark. View is properly titled. At least one CPR box car is on board of the ferry. Photo probably was taken during the 1930s.

C. P. R. CAR FERRIES, WINDSOR, ONT., CANADA

View of Ambassador Bridge at Night, Sandwich, near Windsor, Canada.—26.

Postmark is 1941. Very unusal night photo of the Ambassador Bridge. After the fort at Detroit was built in 1701 by Sieur de Cadillac, the British countered with a town across the river called Sandwich. Just east of Sandwich, a village developed around the ferry dock which provided ferry service to Detroit. It was called Richmond; later its name was changed to Windsor.

No postmark. Four views from Windsor and Detroit are all well captioned. The *S.S. Noronic* was a frequent visitor to this area.

S.S. Noronic, Windsor, Ontario.

C.N.R. Freight Ferry between Windsor and Detroit.

Detroit and Windsor Ferry, Windsor, Canada.

M.C.R. Tunnel between Windsor and Detroit.

No postmark. The three views are self-explanatory. Probably from the late 1930s.

Ambassador Bridge, Windsor, Ontario.

Tunnel Busses, in Detroit-Windsor Tunnel.

Detroit Waterfront from Windsor, Canada.

WINDSOR, Canada

Postmark is 1973. Upper frame reveals a good view of Dieppe Park on the Windsor side and a panoramic view of the Detroit skyline. The lower view is again the Ambassador Bridge.

Postmark is 1907. Real photo showing the *City of Chatham* at the dock next to the Thames lighthouse, which is at the mouth of the Thames River on the north shore of Lake Erie. This boat ran a regular trip between Chatham and Detroit during the summer season.

The Thames Lighthouse and "City of Chatham"

"CITY OF CHATHAM"   LEAVING CHATHAM, ONT.

4066 S

Postmark is 1907. This card shows the *City of Chatham* leaving the dock for the 19 mile trip to the mouth of the river to enter Lake Ste. Clair. Chatham started as a military post in 1793. The name honoured William Pitt, Prime Minister of England, who was the Earl of Chatham. Building smaller lake boats was Chatham's number one industry from 1830 to 1850.

No postmark. The auto in the picture appears to be a late 1920s vintage, so the card is probably from around 1930. The steamer *Thousand Islander* belonging to Canada Steamship Lines is on the Thames River, loaded with passengers. This is probably a day excursion trip.

Steamer "Thousand Islander," Chatham, Ont., Canada.

No postmark. This view of Chatham shows a small dock for smaller boats with a shallow draft that could reach Chatham. The photo is probably from the late 1920s to the early 1930s; it was shot from the opposite direction fo the previous photo.

River Thames from Third Street Bridge, Chatham, Ont., Canada.

HARBOUR ENTRANCE, ERIEAU, ONT.

Postmark is 1943. Although the harbour with two piers looks impressive, it was never a major Great Lakes port. It is situated on Lake Erie south of Chatham. In 1992, population was less than 500. Erieau is better known as a fishing port.

Postmark is 1911. Port Stanley has a long history; it has one of the best harbours on the north shore of Lake Erie. During the early part of the 1900s, it was known for its sandy beaches, a casino and the famous Stork Club, also known as The Pavilion. It attracted all the big bands up until the 1950s. Guy Lombardo's band probably put this community on the map. He played here from 1927 to 1977, shortly before he died. The Pavilion/Stork Club was demolished in 1979. The sender of this card from Port Stanley is interesting; he identified himself as Club Member # 297 of the Halcyion Souvenir Club Exchange and sent the card to an individual in Albuquerque, New Mexico.

THE HARBOUR, PORT STANLEY, ONT.

No postmark. This is a real photograph of the harbour, apparently taken from the same point as the card above. The photographer was closer to the tall structure on the right side of the river, which appears to be a small grain elevator. On the left bank are several boats that appear to be fishing boats. This photo could be from the days when fishing on Lake Erie was a prosperous industry. The closest boat is named the *Stanley Foster*, probably a fishing boat.

Transfer Steamer "Ashtabula". Port Burwell, Ont., Canada

No postmark. The *Ashtabula* was built at St. Clair, Michigan, and was ready for service in 1906. A steel railroad car ferry, it was a joint venture between the CPR in Canada and the Pennsylvania Railway in the USA. The *Ashtabula* carried coal between Ashtabula, Ohio, and Port Burwell, Ontario. Although its coal trade was very profitable, it rarely made much money carrying freight to the USA, because there was very little trade from north to south. After World War II, because of the conversion to diesel engines, the use of coal fell precipitously, and this trans-Lake Erie business was stopped. The boat was taken to Ashtabula on September 29, 1961, and scrapped. (Print quality of card is very poor.)

Postmark is 1908. This is an interesting card because it shows a variety of vessels from a grain boat, a canoe, a yacht, a motor boat and finally a row boat with chairs aft so the honoured guests could ride in comfort!

The Harbor, Port Dover, Canada.

IN THE HARBOR, PORT DOVER, CAN.

Postmark is 1913. Port Dover is located on the north shore of Lake Erie. In 1812, it was known as Dover's Mill and was destroyed by the Americans during the war of 1812. First incorporated as a village and then a town, it was amalgamated in 1974 with two other small towns and now is known as the City of Nanticoke. There is good fishing in the area, especially of perch and pickerel, better known to the southern neighbours as "walleyes." The boat in the photo is the dayliner *Olcott*.

Postmark is 1906. This is a scene along the Port Colborne harbour. There are eight boats and two tugs. Three of the boats have timber as a deck load, illustrating how important the lumber trade was in Canada at the turn of the century. Also note four of the boats are sailing vessels (or have been cut down to barges}. The two tugs are in the foreground.

Port Colborne   Harbor

Postmark is 1908. This scene along the Port Colborne harbour shows a small canaler under full steam. The original grain elevator is on the right. The crane in the foreground belongs to Beattie and Company of Welland, Ontario.

Postmark is 1908. Residual broken ice is near the rear and in front of the two schooners means the photo was taken in late Spring, just before the start of the shipping season. The boat to the left appears to be a wooden steamer. The message on the card sent from Port Colborne to a relative in Seattle, Washington, is interesting: it reports that the young man's injured leg would soon be "put in plaster," allowing him after a long time to be able to sit up! Modern orthopaedic surgery would have him up soon after timely surgery, weight-bearing as tolerated!

No postmark. This card shows the elevator of the Maple Leaf Milling Co., which was founded about 1904, but seems to have originated in a flour mill that began much earlier. Thus the photo on the card is from sometime after 1904, possibly about 1910. The maple leaf name still exist as Maple Leaf Foods, which is the majority owner of Canada Bread and Maple Leaf Bakery, U.S.A.

Canadian Furnace Company, Port Colborne, Ont.

This is a view of the Canadian Furnace Co., situated just south of the Welland Canal on Lake Erie. The first settlers came here from Pennsylvania in the 1780s. In 1834, it was named Port Colborne after Sir John Colborne, Governor General of Canada at that time. Port Colborne became a trading village for boats passing through the Welland canal. Ship's chandlers set up shop here and two railroads came to town. In 1918, a nickel refinery, INCO, built a plant here and refined nickel until 1984; it still refines cobalt and other rare metals today.

Emperor & Midland Prince in Port Colborne Harbor

Date is 1911/12. The boat on the right is the *Emperor*, a grainer built in 1910 for James Playfair of Midland, Ontario and his Inland Line. In 1913, *Emperor* became part of the new CSL fleet. It sailed for 37 years without a mishap. In June 1947, sailing loaded from the Lakehead, she passed Isle Royal and struck Canoe Rocks, where she broke in two. The aft end quickly sank with the engineering crew. The forward end hung up on the rocks for a while, then sank. Total loss of life was 12.

The second boat is the *Midland Prince*, built at Collingwood in 1907. It sailed from 1907 to 1914 for Midland Prince Navigation Company Ltd., when it became part of the CSL fleet. In 1969, it was towed to Spain and scrapped.

No postmark. This is a commemorative card marking the opening of the Welland Canal in 1932. The *Lemoyne*, largest freighter on the Great Lakes at that time, was officially the first freighter to lock through the updated and enlarged canal.

Official Opening of the Welland Canal, Aug. 6, 1932

Freighter "Lemoyne"
Length, 634 feet
Beam, 70 feet
Depth, 29 feet
Wheat Record, 571,885 bushels
Coal capacity, 17,527 tons

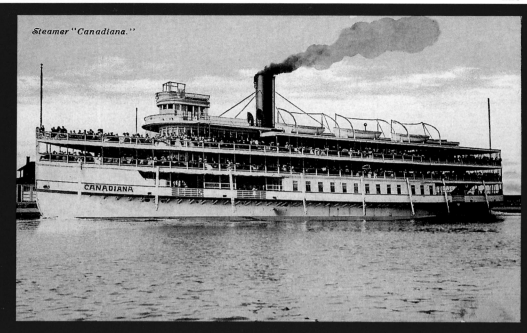

Steamer "Canadiana."

Postmark is 1912. The *Canadiana* was built at Buffalo and launched in 1910. It ran as a dayliner between Buffalo and Crystal Beach, Ontario, until 1955. Attempts were made to save the vessel as a floating museum or restuarant, but the group formed to save it was not successful. The *Canadiana* was scrapped in 2004.

No postmark. This postcard shows the *Americana* leaving Buffalo with a load of passengers heading for Crystal Beach to enjoy the sand and the carnival rides, especially the famous Crystal Beach Cyclone which was built in 1927. This boat, with its sister ship, the *Canadiana*, transported passengers seven months of the year from Buffalo to Crystal Beach. The Cyclone ride was closed in 1946 and transported to a new location in New York State; it is still in use today. Crystal Beach is on the shore of Lake Erie, close to Fort Erie, Ontario.

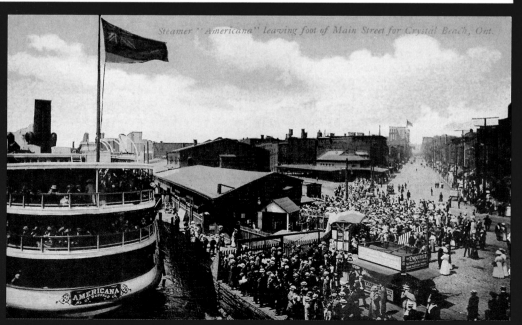

Steamer "Americana" leaving foot of Main Street for Crystal Beach, Ont.

CHAPTER 6

Niagara and Lake Ontario to Kingston

**Niagara Falls • Welland Canal • Queenston • Niagara on the Lake • Lewiston
Port Weller • Port Dalhousie • St. Catharines • Grimsby • Hamilton
Toronto • Port Hope • Cobourg • Trenton • Belleville • Picton • Kingston**

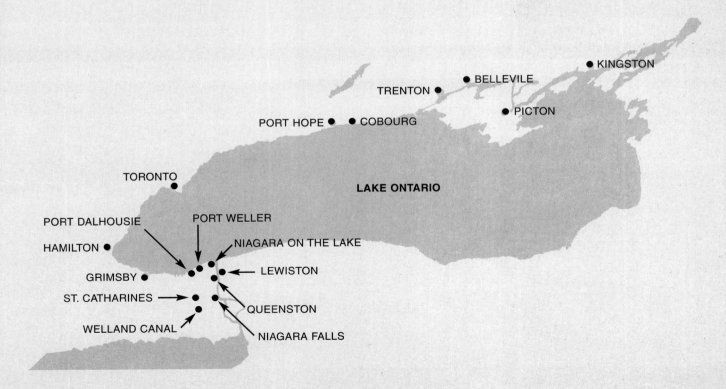

No postmark. The *Maid of the Mist*, the original boat and all its offspring, are probably the most photographed boats on the Great Lakes. There have been nine *Maid of the Mist* boats. The first was launched in 1846, the last in 1997. The original *Maid* was actually a ferry. When the suspension bridge was built over the Niagara River in 1848, the *Maid* became simply a sightseeing boat to allow passengers a close-up view of the Niagara Falls. This photo was probably taken about 1910.

„MAID OF THE MIST" PASSING UNDER STEEL ARCH BRIDGE. 1434

Aqueduct and Ship Canal, Welland, Ontario.

No postmark. Probably published in booklet form with other cards. A specific card could then be torn out, a message written and the card mailed. The city of Welland is on the Welland Ship Canal about midway between Lake Erie and Lake Ontario. The city started about 1788. The first wooden aquaduct that carried the Welland Canal over the Welland River was built in 1829. Prior to 1967, the Welland Canal passed right through the city of Welland. In 1967, a new cut was started, moving the canal 1.5 miles (2.4 km) further east.

No postmark. This appears to be a homemade card. There is no manufacturer's mark on the reverse. Casual observation suggests that the ship in the canal may be a warship, but examination with a magnifying glass points to this vessel as most likely an impressive yacht.

Postmark is 1907. This photo pictures Lock 1 at the northern end of the Welland Canal next to Lake Ontario. The four paintings surrounding the center photo depicts different views of Canada: a Saskatchewan prairie view; the Rockies; the Parliament Buildings in Ottawa, and one of the most photographed sites in the world, Niagara Falls.

Lock No. 3, Welland Ship Canal, near St. Catharines, Ontario. —38.

No postmark. This view is of Lock Number 3 on the Welland Canal. It appears to be a postcard from the late 1930s or early 1940s.

WELLAND CANAL 5   236

This map of the Welland Canal shows the location of the eight locks that were required to step down 326 feet (99.4m) from Lake Erie to the level of Lake Ontario, bypassing the Niagara Falls. The water in the canal flows from south to north.

WELLAND CANAL

The Welland Canal crosses the Niagara Peninsula about 8 miles west of Niagara Falls.

The lift of the Canal is 327 feet, distributed over 8 locks.

The Lake Erie entrance to the Canal is at Port Colborne, about 18 miles west of Buffalo.

The 27 mile Welland Canal overcomes a 326 foot difference in elevation between Lakes Ontario and Erie.

Locks are filled and emptied by gravity flow. Gates, valves and protection fenders are motor driven.

Maximum vessel size: Length 730 feet, beam 75 feet, depth 25.5 feet.

Average lift of lock: 46.5 feet.

Postmark is 1938. Queenston is about 3 miles (4.8 km) north of Niagara Falls in the town of Niagara on the Lake. This is another community started by the United Empire Loyalists who fled the USA after the American revolution in 1774. An American invasion was stopped here during the Queenston Heights battle in the war of 1812, during which the British Major General Isaac Brock was killed. There is an impressive monument on Queenston Heights, commemorating this general. At dock is the steamer *Cayuga* of the CSL line; it ran regularly and for years from Toronto to Queenston.

Steamer Cayuga of Canada Steamship Lines at Queenston Dock.

Troops Disembarking for Niagara Camp

Postmark is 1909. Niagara On The Lake is situated at the mouth of the Niagara River where it flows into Lake Ontario. The conveyances on the dock are all horse-drawn, so the photo was taken before 1909. The boat is the popular dayliner *Cayuga* traveling between Toronto and Niagara On The Lake. The uniforms of the soldiers on the dock make me believe that this photo was taken at the time of the Boer War (1899 to 1902). Niagara On The Lake was a well known location for training soldiers in the Canadian army.

No postmark. This is the only postcard of an American harbour scene that I have included in this book. The historic town of Lewiston saw its first French explorers arrive there in 1615. The community always had close ties with Canada. It is situated directly across from Queenston Heights and Niagara on the Lake, Ontario. Besides a bridge connecting it with Canada, ferries were always available to connect the two foreign shores, the first in 1851 and the last in 1962. The passenger boats out of Toronto and other Lake Ontario ports made Lewiston a stop. This postcard is a testimony to this fact, with the impressive CSL dock being pictured. The undivided back puts the card's date before 1907.

Entering Lock No. 1, New Welland Ship Canal, at Port Weller, Lake Ontario, Canada.

No postmark. Port Weller is at the north end of the Welland Canal on Lake Ontario. It had no natural harbour so the harbour was made by extending an earth embankment out into Lake Ontario for 1.5 miles (2.4km). The town was named after the engineer who supervised the construction of the fourth and final Welland Canal. The canal was started in 1913 and finished in 1932. This photo was taken after 1932; it is probably from the mid 1930s. The boat loaded with passengers appears to be a day liner on an excursion. Port Weller still has an active shipyard.

STEAMER "LAKESIDE" LEAVING PORT DALHOUSIE, ONT.

This is the northern terminus of Welland Canal

1708

Postmark is 1906. As is written on the card, Port Dalhousie was and is the northern terminus of the Welland Canal. The original canal went from Port Dalhousie on Lake Ontario, up Twelve Mile Creek to St. Catharines, ascended the Niagara Escarpment by a lock system to Thorold, and then continued south to Port Colborne on Lake Erie.

No postmark. This is a panoramic view of the Welland canal as it passes by the city of St. Catharines. The first settlers arrived here in the 1780s; they are better known as the United Empire Loyalists. They fought for the British during the Revolutionary War. St. Catharines became a northern terminus for the Underground Railroad from the USA at the time of the American Civil War. This was one entry point for the slaves escaping from the States. During the last century, it was also a major ship building centre on the Great Lakes. Some of the larger boats at that time were built here. The first reference to St. Catharines as an identifiable site was in 1808. (Note: The name of the town is misspelled on the card.)

SECTION OF WELLAND CANAL, FROM THE MOUNTAIN, LOOKING UP THE CANAL. ST. CATHERINES, ONT.

Canadian Revenue Cruiser, St. Catharines, Ont.

No postmark on this nice, sepia-toned postcard. The card is simply titled Canadian Revenue Cutter, but the vessel is the *S.S. Vigilant*. The first Welland Canal was dug in 1824. There were many changes, enlargements and dredgings until the opening of the St. Lawrence Seaway on April 25, 1969.

No postmark. Grimsby Beach started as a summer camp in 1846 and was sponsored by the Methodist Church. It was served by trains and passenger boats. By 1910, the site had evolved into an entertainment complex with midway rides, a "figure eight" roller coaster, a dance pavilion, a theater, and a restaurant. Day liner passenger boats transported the crowds from Hamilton, Toronto and other places. The postcard pictures one such boat, probably the steamer *Macassa*. By the late 1940s, most of the facilities had closed and the site was absorbed by the town of Grimsby.

Waiting for the Passengers, Grimsby Beach, the Pride of Canada

No postmark. There is a message on the reverse side, but the card was never mailed. With the two early flying machines, I would date this card to about 1907 or 1908. Hopefully, the airport from which these machines took off was not far away! This may be a composite card produced by the card company to illustrate a variety of transportation means available at that time!

JUST HAD A GLIMPSE OF THE BEACH ON MY TRIP TO HAMILTON.

"Macassa" passing through the Piers, Hamilton Beach, Canada

Postmark is 1912. This view shows the *Macassa*, a popular day liner, leaving Hamilton harbour after passing through the "piers" at Hamilton Beach.

The name Toronoto is Huron for "meeting place." The original Indian village was located on the east bank at the mouth of the Humber River. The location was very important for the fur traders. Travellers could paddle up the Humber River and then portage to Lake Simcoe. From Lake Simcoe, after a nine-mile portage, they could reach the headwaters of the Nottawasaga River and Georgian Bay. From there, they could even reach the Mississippi River and other points west and south.

The first white man to visit this site was Etienne Brule in 1615. The first railroad to reach Toronto was in 1850. Population growth was steady, but not anything unusual, until after World War II, when the population exploded. First came European immigrants, and later migrants from the Caribbean, Africa and Asia. By 1998, Toronto was the fifth largest city in North America. A few years earlier it overtook Montreal as the largest city in Canada. Although Toronto did not have heavy industries such as the steel mills at Hamilton, it had many diverse industries including banking, financial institutions, manufacturing companies and the most important port on Lake Ontario. It is interesting that most of the postcards of Toronto are views of the lake front prior to World War II. These cards almost always included a view of the Yonge Street Wharf.

TORONTO – WHERE BOATS COME IN

No postmark. Artist-painted card showing the Yonge Street Wharf. Undivided back means it was produced before 1907.

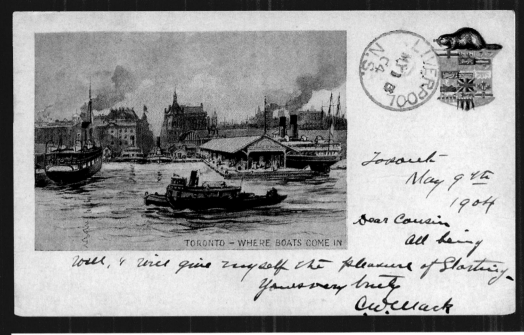

Postmark is 1904. This is the same scene as the previous card, but now it is embellished with the Canadian coat of arms with the beaver over the provincial emblems.

Postmark is 1907. Panoramic view of Toronto from the bay in front of Hanlan's Island, with a ferry heading to the Island.

YONGE STREET DOCK, TORONTO.

No postmark. The scene is probably after World War I. Again we see the Yonge St Wharf. The steamer *Cambria* is on the left. In the far background is the aft end of another boat, which could be the *Rochester* or *Toronto*. These two sister ships sailed out of Toronto for many years.

No postmark. This is same as the card above except the publisher cropped it differently, cutting off the name of the *Cambria*.

HARBOR TORONTO CANADA.

No postmark. Water front scene, probably about 1920. The boats are not identifiable.

No postmark. Another view of the foot of Yonge Street. Photographs of this area probably made up the vast majority of postcards sold in Toronto until the CN Tower was built in 1976. The boat docked to the right with the two smoke stacks could be the *Cayuga*.

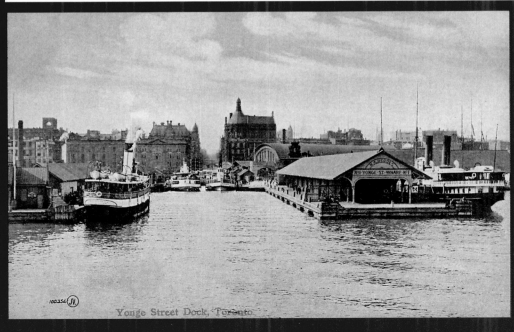

No postmark. Same old scene showing boats around the Yonge Street Wharf. A variation on a theme: this card is embellished with a white rose and a butterfly!

Harbor, Toronto, Canada.

Yonge Street Dock, Toronto, Canada.

Postmark is not clear. Another view of the harbour, showing the slip between piers at the Yonge Street docks. The boat cannot be identified with certainty.

This postcard is by the artist Charles F. Flowers. The *S.S. Kingston* is in the foreground. It traveled between Niagara on the Lake and Montreal with stops at Toronto and Hamilton. The *Kingston* was built in 1901; it became part of the CSL fleet in 1913 and then spent the remainder of its career sailing between Toronto, the Thousand Islands and Kingston, Ontario. Its last trip was on September 17, 1949, the day the *Noronic* burnt at Toronto Harbour. It was scrapped at Hamilton in 1950. Undivided back dates the card before 1907.

No postmark. Another scene at the Yonge St. Wharf, probably early 1920s. The boat is not identified.

Arrival of Niagara Boat at Toronto, Canada

5123. Niagara Navigation Co.'s Ship "Cayuga" connecting Buffalo, Niagara Falls, Toronto.

Postmark is 1915. The popular *S.S. Cayuga* is shown approaching a crowded pier in Toronto, its decks lined with people ready to embark on the very popular run to Port Dalhousie. (Print quality is very poor.)

No postmark. This sepia-toned card was copyrighted in 1919, dating the photo some time before that year. It was taken from an "aeroplane," which makes it an unusual and rare card. I am certain that intensive research would identify the the larger boats.

WATERFRONT, TORONTO, ONT., FROM AN AEROPLANE
COPYRIGHT, CANADA, 1919 BY CANADIAN POST CARD CO., TORONTO

This postcard reproduces a photo that was taken in 1926 of the construction of the "Terminal Warehouse" on Toronto's harbour front. The card is a free card advertising the new Queen's Quay Terminal. The warehouses have been redeveloped into a new retail outlets and restaurants complex called "Queen's Quay Terminal". The postcard is quite recent.

"*Fulfillment is coming back to the origin with the added experience of the way.*"

Anon.

Toronto Harbour showing Royal York Hotel. —40

No postmark. This is a view that includes the Royal York Hotel built by the CPR in 1929. The hotel is still very exclusive; it has been completely refurbished and now is managed by the Fairmont Hotel Chain of the USA. The larger boat in the left background appears to be the *Noronic*. The card is probably from the late 1930s or early 1940s.

Postmark is 1958. This is a photograph of one of the ferries that connected the mainland with the three Toronto Islands. Note how drastically the skyline has changed after World War II.

The Harbour, Port Hope, Ont.

Postmark is 1936. This is a real photo of Port Hope harbour. The building complex on the left is the "Port Hope Sanitary Manufacturing Company." There are no boats and very little activity. This photo may have been taken a few years before or during the Great Depression! Magnification reveals three vehicles parked near the building on the left; one is a coupe with a rumble seat, which fits in with an early 1930s auto. The site of Port Hope was originally an Indian village; it sits on a river that was a canoe highway leading to Rice Lake. The United Empire Loyalists arrived here from the USA in1793. The town was named after Colonel Henry Hope, a former Lt. Governor of Quebec.

THE HARBOUR, COBOURG ONT.

No postmark. This scene, judging by the dress of a lady in the right foreground, puts it into the early part of the century. Cobourg was founded by United Empire Loyalists in 1798. First named Amherst, its name was changed to Cobourg in 1918 to honour Princess Charlotte's marriage to Prince Leopold of Saxony Cobourg. Victoria College, now part of the University of Toronto, started in Cobourg. The actress Marie Dressler was born here in 1868; by age 14 she was off to Broadway. Paul Kane, famous western American artist born in Ireland, was raised here. He painted western scenes for the Hudson Bay Company. The large vessel at dock, with flags flying, is not identified, nor are the schooners.

Postmark is 1907. A panoramic view of Trenton harbour with two boats at dock. The larger one is the sidewheeler *Alexandria*, which plied Lake Ontario carrying freight and passengers. She was built in 1866 at Hull, Quebec. She was lost in a gale in 1915 at the Scarborough Bluffs near Toronto. The boat belonged to the Ontario and Quebec Navigation Company, which was part of the CSL.

TRENTON, ONT (THE HARBOUR & SOUTHERN OUTLET OF THE TRENT VALLEY CANAL.)

Twelve O'Clock Point Summer Resort, Trenton, Ontario.

Postmark is 1908. This is a view of a small passenger boat embarking and disembarking passengers at a summer tourist resort, probably on the Trent-Severn Canal, now called the Trent-Severn Waterway. The city of Trenton is located at the outlet of this waterway where it exits into Lake Ontario. The canal starts at Port Severn on Georgian Bay. Trenton was founded in 1790, and by 1800 it was a major lumber and industrial centre. It became a city in 1980 and, after amalgamating with three townships, is now known as the City of Quinte West.

Postmark is 1906. This is a view of Queen Victoria Park with the City of Belleville in the background. Belleville has an excellent yacht and small recreational boat harbour, which never accommodated large Great Lakes steamers. The city was settled by united Empire Loyalists in1784.

Queen Victoria Park, Belleville, Canada

Postmark is 1912. This view is taken from the same vantage point as the previous card, showing Queen Victoria Park.

Victoria Park,   Belleville, Ont.

No postmark. Title is self-explanatory. The actual harbour would be in the distant background. Note the closest bridge is a pedestrian foot bridge. This photo was probably taken before 1910.

Bridges over Moira River, Belleville, Ont., Canada

103,301.

The postmark is 1930. This card, although postmarked 1930, probably came from an earlier date. There are no large vessels. I do not believe Belleville was known as a major lake port. The card is a painting by an unknown artist.

The Harbour, Belleville, Ont., Canada.

Postmark is 1908. This scene is near Picton, with three day liners loading passengers for a summer outing. The left boat is the *Brockville*, the middle boat is the *Aletha*, and the boat to the right is the *Vadora*. Picton was incorporated as a village in 1837. It was named after after Sir General Thomas Picton, who was General Wellington's second in command at the Battle of Waterloo. Sir John A. MacDonald, the first Prime Minister of Canada, managed a law firm in Picton for his uncle.

Picton Harbour, Ont, Canada.

The postmark is 1921. The loaded boat approaching the dock is the *Aletha*. Other boats are not identified. It appears that the day liner is returning people after their cruise and soon will take on a new bunch!

Postmark is 1906. This panoramic view of Kingston shows the main harbour for the lake boats in the background. Kingston is at the southern terminus of the Rideau Canal System, which started at Bytown (now Ottawa, the capital of Canada). The threat that the Americans could block the St. Lawrence caused the British to built a fort at the site of Fort Fronenac, which had been built here by the French in 1673. In 1758, during the Seven Years War, the British captured the fort from the French and renamed it Kingston. Commercial ship building was always important here. Kingston became a British military centre. The first Canadian Parliament opened here in 1841, but was moved to Ottawa in 1844.

Kingston, Ontario, Grand Trunk Railway System

Postmark is 1908. The view is from Wolfe Island looking towards Kingston. Champlain was probably the first European to see and traverse the island after he and his band of Huron warriors successfully raided the Iroquois near Lake Champlain. Wolfe Island was called Ile Grande by The French until 1792, when the English changed the name to Wolfe Island. It is the largest of the 1,000 Islands and is now mostly cultivated. The island is a prime site for tourism, and a regular ferry service is maintained from the mainland.

Kingston Harbor from Wolfe Island, Kingston, Canada

Postmark 1908. This photo shows part of the original fortifications built by the British in Kingston harbour.

Kingston's Fortifications.

CHAPTER 7

St. Lawrence River to Montreal

**Gananoque • Brockville • Prescott • Cornwall • Lachine Rapids
Montreal**

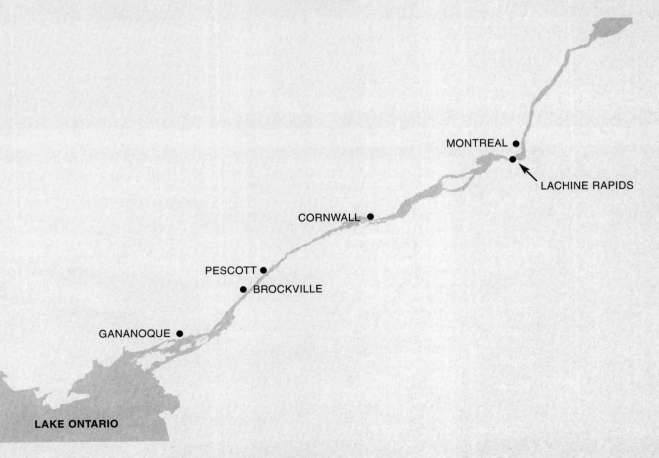

MONTREAL ●

LACHINE RAPIDS

CORNWALL ●

PESCOTT ●
● BROCKVILLE

GANANOQUE ●

LAKE ONTARIO

No postmark. Real photo by R.N. McClung, probably from the early part of the last century. Gananoque is opposite the Thousand Islands; its name is Indian meaning "the place of peace". It is situated where the Gananoque River flows into the St. Lawrence River. The founder of the town was Joel Stone, a British Empire Loyalist who came from Connecticut. Because of its location at the confluence of two rivers, abundant water power was available, and many factories were built here. Undivided back; the card is before 1907.

No postmark. For years, The *Champion* was used as a ferry running in the Thousand Islands between Gananoque, Ontario and Clayton, New York. Since the Thousand Islands Bridge was opened in 1939, the ferry obviously operated before that time and the postcard is probably from the 1930s.

No postmark. The card shows the steamer *Toronto,* which belonged to the Richelieu and Ontario Navigation Company, near Brockville on the St. Lawrence River. This steamboat ran for years between Montreal and Toronto during the summer months.

Steamer Toronto passing up the St. Lawrence River,   Brockville, Ont., Canada.

Postmark is 1933. This photo shows the *S.S. Toronto* at Prescott after taking on more passengers. The vessel would proceed to Montreal, arriving there for an overnight stay. Prescott was founded in 1810. Prior to the building of the St. Lawrence Seaway, it was the only deepwater port between Toronto and Montreal.

Postmark is 1934. This large grain elevator was built in Prescott because it was the only deepwater port between Toronto and Montreal. The grain boats from the Upper Lakes could unload here and the "salties" would transport grain and other freight across the Atlantic. After the opening of the St. Lawrence Seaway, this factor became less important, because the ocean-going freighters could go all the way to the Lakehead, load cargo, and then via the Seaway sail directly to foreign ports without transferring their cargo.

New Terminal Elevator Capacity 5,000,000 Bushels, Prescott, Ont.

No postmark. This is a view of a boat, probably a ferry, approaching Prescott, Ontario. The card appears to be # 5 of an inexpensive postcard series probably intended for the tourist trade. It seems to be from the 1930s. (Very poor quality print.)

St. Lawrence River at Prescott, Ontario.—5.

Locks on the Cornwall Canal near Cornwall, Ont.

108501 JV

No postmark. View of the locks at Cornwall, probably taken during the 1920s, well before the Seaway was built. Only a "canaller" could navigate through the original St. Lawrence Canal and lock system. Remember that, when the C.P.R. had the *Keewatin* and *Assiniboia* built in Scotland, the ships had to be cut in two before traversing the St. Lawrence lock system. They were then rejoined at a Buffalo shipyard before reaching their destination of Owen Sound. These vessels were about 346 feet in length. The city of Cornwall was settled by United Empire Loyalists in 1784; it has developed into an industrial and manufacturing centre.

Postmark is not clear. The stamp has a likeness of King George V, so the card is after 1911. The view is of the locks just above Cornwall, Ontario.

The Locks above Cornwall, Ont., Can.

NADA STEAMSHIP LINES

No postmark. This photo was taken in 1958, at the Long Sault Rapids, before the St. Lawrence Seaway opened. The canaller pictured is a small oil tanker. During the early 1800s, no one was certain if it was safe to "shoot" the rapids with a bigger boat. In 1840, local Indians were paid $1,000.00 to test the rapids on the south side with a 40-foot square crib with stakes protruding downward. No stakes were broken, proving the rapids navigable. In 1848, a vessel called *George Frederic* went down the north channel, taking only 25 minutes to traverse 12 miles. It became quite popular to "shoot the rapids" in larger passenger boats, and many vessels were built for this purpose, the last being the *Rapids Queen* in 1910.

No postmark. Since the *Fairmount* was cut down to a barge in 1963, this real photo was taken before then. The *Fairmount* was built in 1913 in Scotland. It was typical of the canaller's size, weighing 1,851 gross tons. The size and design of the canallers was determined by the size and shape of Lock # 17 at Cornwall before the St. Lawrence Seaway was completed. The bottom breadth of the canal was 43 feet and 8 inches; it had a draft of 14 feet. The canallers were designed to fit these measurements. The *Fairmount* continued working as a barge until 1970, when it was broken up for scrap metal at Sorel, Quebec.

Lachine is synonymous with its name-sake, the Lachine Rapids. I felt since "shooting the rapids" was such a popular activity not only for the average tourist but for anyone wanting a thrill with an element of danger, I have selected eight postcards from my collection to illustrate this popular attraction. This first card has no postmark. It shows the *Str. Gatineau* of 175 net tons shooting the rapids. This boat was built in 1873 at Quebec City. Later it became the *Str. Paul Smith*. The boat was piloted by a local Indian who knew where all the dangerous rocks were located. Shooting the boiling rapids provided a great thrill for the passengers, and the boat would do this once a day during the summer season.

Postmark is 1901. This "Oilette" card with the painting of the *Sovereign* shooting the Rapids is by Charles Flower. The *Sovereign* was built at Montreal in 1889 and was 303 net tons.

Postmark is 1906. The card shows the *Algerian* in the rapids. The boat was built in 1875 and eventually sunk at Split Rock with the loss of several lives. This proved that the "shooting of the rapids" was not without risk!

Steamer "Algerian" Running Long Sault Rapids, St. Lawrence River

STEAMER PRESCOTT IN LACHINE RAPIDS

Postmark is 1905. This card is of the *Prescott*, a side wheeler doing its thing. This boat was about 400 gross tons and ran from Montreal to Prescott, carrying passengers on a regular over-night schedule. Many of the other boats would do only day trips, shoot the rapids, and return to Montreal.

Navigation Co.'s Steamer
" Empress "
Shooting Lachine Rapids Montreal

No postmark. The card shows the *Empress* of 410 net tons shooting the rapids. It was built in Montreal in 1875 and was launched as the *Peerless*.

Postmark is 1908. Card shows the *Corsican* running the rapids. This side wheeler was built in 1870 in Montreal and had a gross tonnage of 478.

Shooting Lachine Rapids, Montreal.

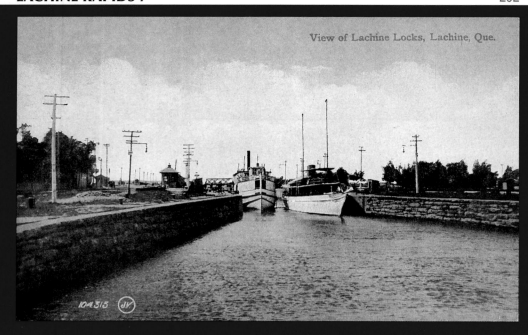

View of Lachine Locks, Lachine, Que.

Postmark is 1913. This is a view of the Lachine locks at Lachine., Quebec. Lachine is part of Montreal and had always been important for the locks named after the community. The Lachine Canal extends for 14.5 km from the "old Port" of Montreal to Lake St. Louis. It opened for shipping in 1825 and was closed in 1970 with the opening of the St. Lawrence Seaway. The canal bypassed the Lachine Rapids. After 1970, the canal banks were used for recreation by hikers and bikers. In 2002, the canal was reopened for pleasure craft only. The postcard shows at least two boats locking through; one appears to be a small freighter or fishing boat, while the other vessel is definitely a private yacht.

Postmark is 1945. The *Rapids King* is shown shooting the rapids but Cornwall is not close to the Lachine Rapids, so there is an error in the caption. Judging from the number of passengers, this was a day trip for the thrill of "shooting the rapids."

Rapid's King shooting Lachine Rapids near Cornwall, Ont — 3799

No postmark. This photo probably was taken from in front of the Bon Secours Church, possibly even from below the cupola; it shows what a busy place the Montreal harbour was. There are no motor cars or trucks, so this photo dates before 1905.

Montreal. Harbour

MONTREAL. The Harbour

No postmark. This card was produced by Rafael Tuck and Sons of England, who published postcards from 1900 to the early 1920s. Their cards are well done, with good detail. All conveyances in the photo are horse drawn, with no autos or trucks in sight; so the photo probably was taken before 1905. Note the "Sailors' Church" in the left background.

Postmark is 1905. There are four ocean freighters, one large St .Lawrence type steamer, one smaller steamer and four vessels with masts for sails visible to the left. In the right background is the dome of Notre Dame de Bon Secours.

MONTREAL   Birdseye View of the Harbour   Illustrated Post Card Co.. Montreal 722

HARBOR MONTREAL.

No postmark. This is a panoramic view of the docks and the harbour. Most of the conveyances are horse drawn except for one electric street car. There may be one horse drawn car in front of the electric streetcar, which dates the pictures between 1892 to 1894. Horse drawn streetcars were discontinued in 1892, and the conversion to electric was completed by 1894. In the right foreground is a partial view of the church of Notre Dame de Bon Secours, also known as the "Sailors' Church".

Montreal Harbour

No postmark. This is another early view of Montreal harbour. The publisher is The Valentine and Sons card company in Great Britian. The photographer, James Valentine, was a well known Scot who produced a lot of cards for the Canadian and American market until the 1920s. Then the company was sold and eventually became part of a Scottish card company that is still producing postcards today.

This photo shows a busy scene at Montreal harbour. There are no motor vehicles, dating the photo before 1905. A long line of horse drawn taxis is waiting to pick up passengers from the large passenger vessels in the left foreground.

Postmark is 1907. The card is identified as a view at Windmill Point in Montreal Harbour. The elevator belongs to the Grand Trunk Railway, which sprung up as a competitor to the CPR, but went into receivership and then became part of the new entity started by the Canadian Government, the CNR. Besides the six barges and two tugs, there is a dayliner and one freighter at dock.

GRAND TRUNK ELEVATOR, WINDMILL POINT, MONTREAL.

75:—Harbour   Montreal   le port

No postmark. The card is a view of part of the Montreal harbour with two oceangoing ships at dock. This inexpensive card of the 1930s is not a good reproduction.

No postmark. This domestic card is not of good quality with poor definition of the buildings in the background. It is obviously a winter scene and the automobile models are from the 1930s. The vessel is not identified.

Le Port de Montréal, Canada.—The Harbour.—83.

No postmark. This is a panoramic view of Montreal, looking west from Mount Royal. The St. Lawrence River and the Victoria Bridge are in the background.

131—Looking West, Montréal.
Vue de l'Ouest.

No postmark. This steel bridge was the first direct link from Montreal to the south shore of the St. Lawrence River and to the USA. It was built in 1859 by the Grand Trunk Railway as a covered bridge. The steam locomotives running through it producd so much gas, smoke and steam - making the passengers uncomfortable - that it was converted to an open bridge in 1896. Named after Queen Victoria, the bridge continues in operation today as a railway and automobile crossing.

No postmark. This is a collection card printed by the Steamship Historcal Society of America, Inc. The boat is the *Quebec*, built in 1928 by the Davis Shipbuilding Co. in Quebec for the St. Lawrence and Saguenay cruises. The photo shows it at dock in Montreal. In 1950, while at Tadoussac, it was set on fire by an arsonist just after leaving the dock. The captain and crew bravely took the boat back to Tadoussac and ran it aground near a pier. Everyone was saved except one family, who against the captain's order, returned to the passenger deck to retrieve their personal belongings and were lost in the fire.

No postmark. The card's caption is self-explanatory. The boat is probably a day liner. The photo is a real photo. Judging from its appearance, it seems to me that this boat was not a rapids-traversing vessel.

Short pleasure cruises on the St. Lawrence River.

References and Bibliography

Rev. Peter Van Der Linden, Editor: *Great Lakes Ships We Remember*, 1979, and *Great Lakes Ships We Remember II*, 1984. Both volumes published by Freshwater Press Inc., Cleveland, Ohio. These publications are under the auspices of the Marine Historical Society of Detroit.

Bowen, Thomas Dana: *Lore of the Lakes*, 1940.

Bowen, Thomas Dana: *Memories of the Lakes*, 1946.

Barry, James P.: *Georgian Bay, An Illustrated History*, 1992.

Barry, James P.: *Ships of the Great Lakes, 300 Years of Navigation*, 1973.

Ashdown, Dana: *Railway Steamships of Ontario*, 1988. *Inland Seas*, Quarterly Journal of the Great Lakes Historical Society.

John M. Mills: *Canadian Coastal and Inland Steam Vessels 1809-1930, The Steamship Historical Societyof America*, 1979.

James Lewis Lowe: *Standard Postcard Catalog*, 1982.

Inland Seas, quarterly journal of the Great Lakes Historical Society, Vermilion, Ohio; various volumes.

Huronia Museum, Midland, Ontario: 61 postcards of Great Lakes Harbour Scenes.

Owen Sound Marine Museum, Owen Sound: 4 postcards, including the book's cover image.

Multiple Websites and their multiple links, too numerous to list.